W9-AEZ-558

THE
UNFINISHED
SOCIETY

E169.1
B7553

THE UN- FINISHED SOCIETY

by HERBERT VON BORCH

translated by Mary Ilford

1963

APR

foreword by MAX LERNER 78496

HAWTHORN BOOKS, INC.   PUBLISHERS

NEW YORK

Copyright © 1962 by R. Piper & Co. Verlag, Munich, Germany. Copyright under International and Pan American Copyright Conventions. All rights reserved, including the right to reproduce this book, or portions thereof, in any form, except for the inclusion of brief quotations in a review. All inquiries should be addressed to Hawthorn Books, Inc., 70 Fifth Avenue, New York City 11. This book was manufactured in the United States of America and was published simultaneously in Canada by McClelland & Stewart, Ltd., 25 Hollinger Road, Toronto 16. It was originally published in Germany under the title *Amerika: Die unfertige Gesellschaft,* © 1960 by R. Piper & Co. Verlag. Library of Congress Catalogue Card Number 62-15688. Suggested Decimal Classification: 136.4.

FIRST EDITION
October, 1962

Foreword

IT IS a delight to have a knowing account of contemporary trends in our American culture written from the perspective of an able German newspaperman. It adds notably to the tradition of foreign commentators on the American personality and culture. In its original form, as *Die Unfertige Gesellschaft,* this book served to introduce the new America to a large German and European audience. In its present form, updated to take advantage of the most recent literature, it can serve as a mirror which Americans can hold up and see things about themselves which they might otherwise miss by taking them for granted.

Let us face it: just as there is an emerging Soviet man, Chinese man, African man—yes, and European man—so there is an emerging America and American. I cannot say that I share all the nuances of the author's interpretations as he traces the new American and the new America; but as a laborer for many years in the same vineyard, I bear testimony to his industry and skill. It is moreover, in the deepest sense, a revolutionary America of which he has written. Whatever the "deification" the American accords his society, it is not a completed or frozen society but one in constant—almost volcanic—flow of inner change. My own experience, with a book that stretched over a decade in the writing, was that by the time I had completed a first draft the dynamism of change forced me to rewrite a number of sections, lest they seem archaic. Mr. von Borch has shown courage in singling out for intensive treatment some of the aspects of American life which, by the fact of being most responsive to change, are therefore also the most perishable aspects.

I cite his perceptive discussion of the Beatniks, of American pressures toward conformity, of "group ethics," of television and its current forms, of recent educational trends, of the struggle for desegregation, of the massive problems of leisure, of the power elite, of alienation, of the American attitudes toward erotic expressiveness. It is a perilous thing to write about the emerging American, far more perilous than in De Tocqueville's day because everything today moves faster, but Mr. von Borch has had the hardihood to brave the perils. In the process he has seen America not (as so many European travelers have done) as the tail of the European dog, nor as a monstrous chimaera fit for no habitation, animal or human, but as a characteristic civilization of its own which is yet subject to the storms, erosions and fires operative in the world as a whole.

The problem of every writer on America is the temptation to be caught up and lost in the vast but deceptive literature of American self-criticism which is pouring out of every university, every novelist's study. For there is always a double problem to be faced: not only what is wrong with America, but how and why—with so many things incontestably wrong— it manages to survive and in some ways even to thrive. The flux of American life is there, yes; but the frame is also there within which alone all the flux has some meaning. De Tocqueville's greatness lay not so much in his discerning of the flux, although he was one of the first to note the desperate restlessness of Americans: it lay in his sure *placing of the frame*—the passions, the grandeurs and the miseries of egalitarian democracy. He had no psychological monographs or sociological treatises on mass culture, mass leisure, mass loneliness, the power elite, the organization man, the alienated intellectual, the military-industrial complex, to read and absorb. He relied on his notebooks in which he had scribbled the notes of his talks with the humble as well as the great, and he relied on his own uncanny awareness of the clamor and claims within the breasts of men at the time, in Europe as in America.

Von Borch has a frame too, although (as with most contemporary books on America) it is harder to define it. He sees the present era as marking the end of American innocence in the sense of the great American dream of Utopianism and human perfectibility, and the new critical realism with which Americans today regard the world and their own role in it. "The great privilege of the Americans," De Tocqueville wrote, "does not simply consist in their being more enlightened than other nations, but in their being able to repair the faults they may commit." It is this "self-correcting" quality of American life, as von Borch puts it in speaking of the American economy, which furnishes the larger frame within which American self-criticism is best viewed. He sees that the "permeable state" is still tough enough to make a strong bid to become the viable state; that the alienated intellectuals have become largely reconciled with their country and their culture without ceasing to be critical and even intellectually rebellious.

Hence the American story is not wholly told on the pages of history, the book is not closed, even the current chapter is not yet written. It is in this sense, most deeply, that America is *the unfinished society* which von Borch has so admirably delineated. The energies of the world still flow to it, and its own energies still flow outward to the world.

MAX LERNER

Table of Contents

1.

Farewell to Utopia: An Introduction

NATIONS, and the social fabric they develop, are the product of accident and necessity, of far-off causes and inescapable pressures—with one exception. That exception is the United States of America. The United States did not evolve, it was not woven in the uneven, confused pattern of history like other nations. It was created.

Before America was a nation, it was an experiment, an idea, a plan, a Utopia, a promise, a dream. It has never ceased to be all these, or to desire to be all these; it has never desired completion. Today, however, the pressure of global rivalry between two socio-religious systems with opposing political principles is forcing America to this realization: that while it has prospered as a nation beyond all measure, beyond anything conceivable at the time of its first beginnings on the empty North Atlantic coast, its Utopia, its dream, the idea which gave it birth, has collapsed. For the first time in the nearly four centuries of the American experiment, America as a nation is encountering failure, that final frontier of every civilization. It has reached the termination of boundless potentiality. It is beginning to find out—and the discovery comes as no small shock—that the optimism on which it had always fed, an optimism without a countervailing sense of the tragic, is not enough.

America is beginning to see that the unprecedented material success it has achieved is a mixed blessing; that this success bears the seeds of its own destruction. A reevaluation of basic values seems to be imminent. The best minds in the country know that the American dream has spent itself and that the nation must live without it. The people at large have barely realized this as yet, but they will. For of course it is not America, or the American people, or the American nation, that has failed. American society possesses virtually inexhaustible capacities for self-redress. The loose, flexible form of government and social structure which it has developed provide it with the greatest possible scope for nondogmatic change. At the same time, it has wisely established conservative restraints against any over-hasty or partisan solution. But now the American nation must take leave of its Utopia. Should that Utopia be retained as an ideology without basis in reality, it could easily degenerate into a collective deception. America will finally have to bid farewell to the eighteenth century.

Only in American civilization do we find the great and stirring currents of the eighteenth century projected so forcibly into the actualities of the twentieth century. Because in the second half of that century, in 1776 to be precise, a colonial venture was transformed into a free, independent society by a deliberate and well-pondered act of will, and because the Union was not so much born as made, America more than any other historical entity can be identified with a particular philosophy. Its Utopia, which the Founding Fathers wished to achieve for all time on North American soil, flowed from the religion of freedom, as Croce calls that fusion of ideas and sentiments known to the history of philosophy as enlightenment, rationalism, optimism or deism.

In the generation of the Founding Fathers, these philosophical ideas engendered social institutions, and the identity between thought and action became fact in a short, creative moment which laid the foundations of America. Thomas Jefferson, Alexander Hamilton, James Madison, John Adams, Benjamin Franklin (that father of all Yankees, as Carlyle dubbed him) and Thomas Paine were at once politicians and theorists in their own right. The Declaration of Independence, which Jefferson drafted, was as much a revolutionary act of liberation as it was the first manifesto of philosophical Americanism. Its message is the eighteenth-century message of the unlimited capacity of man, as a free being, to create his own social system and to recreate it as often as it fails to satisfy the two values which Jefferson considered paramount—freedom and happiness.

The decisive words are: "We hold these truths to be self-evident: that all men are created equal, that they are endowed by their Creator with certain unalienable rights, that among these are life, liberty and the pursuit of happiness. That to secure these rights, governments are instituted among men, deriving their just powers from the consent of the governed; that whenever any form of government becomes destructive of these ends, it is the right of the people to alter or abolish it, and to institute new government . . ."

The most widely-read, non-American political philosopher at the time was Adam Ferguson of Edinburgh, who wrote in 1767: "We speak of art as distinguished from nature; but art itself is natural to man. He is in some measure the artificer of his own frame, as well as of his fortune, and is destined, from the first age of his being, to invent and contrive . . ." Here, in anticipation, we find the characteristically American linking of freedom with rational action (the latter conceived of as the unlimited power of applied science). In a letter which Jefferson wrote from Monticello ten days before his death, this link is graphically expressed: "The general spread of the light of science has already laid open to every view the palpable truth that the mass of mankind has not been born with saddles on their backs, nor a favoured few booted and spurred, ready to ride them . . ."

The individual American states came into being by a deliberate act of their peoples; here too the principle obtained that

even sovereign states can be "made." When the thirteen colonies declared themselves independent states in 1776, the
colonial charters, as Bryce wrote in his famous *American
Commonwealth,* became "naturally the State constitution." But
it was not "naturally" in the sense that the states were the
product of some blind force of history. A state constitution,
in Bryce's words, "is really nothing but a law made directly
by the people voting at the polls . . . Hence the enactment of
a constitution is an exercise of direct popular sovereignty to
which we find few parallels in modern Europe . . ." There
are in fact no parallels, for the Swiss cantons—the only
parallel Bryce suggests—are much too small to be really
comparable.

Even before the French Revolution, the Declaration of
Human and Civil Rights in 1789, which was inspired by the
Bill of Rights of the American states in 1776, the emergence
of the "sovereign" individual states was indissolubly linked
with the fundamental right to personal liberty. Although the
Declaration of Independence speaks of "self-evident" truths,
the enumeration of the citizen's fundamental rights in the individual states was basically religious. Human rights were
regarded as given before the existence of the state; that is
precisely why they are inalienable. God created men free and
equal. Rational enlightenment as the religion of freedom: that
is the philosophical root of Americanism. That is the mixture
of reason and belief that fed the American Utopia.

For all their differences, intellectually the Founding Fathers
were men of their century. From them the great eighteenth-
century ideas flowed down to the people, losing their
transcendental content on the way and declining into the
light-hearted optimism which is at the basis of the accepted
ideology of progressive perfectibility. In this connection, an
interesting comparison suggests itself between the founding of
the North American states and the outbreak of the French
Revolution, the two events of major historical significance

that took place in the latter part of the eighteenth century. For while the order introduced in 1789 with such éclat has suffered continual mutation ever since, the order introduced so much more soberly in 1776 has been preserved to this day. Only in America has there ever been a society created—and maintained—on the basis of a philosophy—the optimistic philosophy of progress. As Alfred Weber writes: "That period saw the full emergence of the dangerous optimism which makes the eighteenth century immortal. It consists in the notion of human perfectibility, in the idea that man is capable of achieving perfection by means of what was called 'enlightenment.'" The principle that man by nature possesses the capacity to be free, to decide freely among various alternatives, to choose, for the first and only time in human history and on American soil, was the foundation of a state. That principle underlies the American dream, the Utopia without which America long believed—almost to this day—that it could not live.

The very word "Utopia," formed of two Greek words meaning "nowhere," was coined shortly after the discovery of America. In 1516, Sir Thomas More wrote the book he called *Utopia,* in which he described what he regarded as an ideal social and economic system. Although he did not mention America as such, his contemporaries had no doubt that he had located his earthly paradise—where men lived in happy leisure, albeit under medieval monastic discipline—in that new, indeterminate region far to the west which the Discoverer had introduced to the European consciousness. The undreamed-of prospect of unexplored lands where a new and better human society could be created, the thought that paradise was perhaps not lost after all, stimulated the spirit of social reform. And one hundred and twenty-eight years later there began, with the Pilgrim Fathers, the long series of settlements, founded in protest against their abandoned homeland, which were to be self-contained little Utopias in practice.

There were about one hundred such communities, mainly primitive Christian settlements of varying duration (some, like the Amana community of Iowa, have survived right up to the present) comprising in all about 100,000 persons: Harmonists, Separatists, Perfectionists, Transcendentalists and so on. In an extreme form, they expressed what America meant to all the streams of immigrants that have flowed across the ocean for three centuries.

Even if the motives of the settlers were often very obvious and not always noble, the majority of those who freely left the old continent for the sake of an untamed, uncivilized new world were drawn by the living Utopia which people call "the American dream."

This dream, which drew people like a magnet to settle the empty lands, is also the dominant structural element of America. This is so despite all the pessimism about and criticism of their society voiced by native intellectuals, to which that society has remained all but impervious. From the dream stemmed the notion that optimism, faith in the promised land, and satisfaction in belonging to it was a patriotic duty. Jefferson himself shared this fundamental American enthusiasm. In his inaugural address as President, in 1801, he said: "Kindly separated by nature and a wide ocean from the exterminating havoc of one quarter of the globe . . . possessing a chosen country, with room enough for our descendants to the thousandth and thousandth generation . . . what more is necessary to make us a happy and prosperous people? Still one thing more . . . a wise and frugal Government . . ." In the eyes of Jefferson and of America, said one commentator, God seemed to have abandoned that far-off "quarter of the globe," that ancient Europe, like Sodom and Gomorrah. The Americans were the people of the ark.

This sense of escape is an essential part of the American dream. It sustained the optimistic mood of the American experiment—only temporarily disturbed by the depression of the thirties—up to the opening of the post-World War II period. Then, only fragmentarily perceived, it began to fade. Now, in the sixties, America has to reassemble the fragments and see what can be saved. It is a sobering, healing awakening, whose consequences are impossible to predict. No people, it seems, may live forever with Utopia.

That unmistakably American concept of foreign policy, isolationism—the deliberate refusal to become involved in the power conflicts of the world which Americans had just escaped and in all "entangling alliances" which might involve them again—was a logical consequence of the dream. The firm belief in America's geographical withdrawal was the condition for building a better world. To protect this withdrawal by means of foreign policy was the essence of statecraft. Louis J. Halle, who was a member of the Policy Planning Staff of the State Department before entering upon his academic career, calls this a "philosophical isolationism." This philosophical isolationism, writes Halle in *Dream and Reality,* "was profound and meaningful. It represented a purpose for which America was created. It represented a national outlook, the dream of Utopia which had brought so large and hopeful a population across the seas from the Old World. Therefore the passing of this traditional isolationism in its degree can mean nothing less than the defeat of the dream. It represents the triumph of reality over the ideal . . ." Since the cold war with the Soviet Union, since the revolution in weapon technology of the nuclear age, since the onset of world-wide conflict for the political soul of the developing nations and the race for the conquest of space, America can no longer be a type of Noah's ark, borne by God's grace upon the waters of the flood.

We could put it this way. Until a short time ago, the American Utopia had not been contradicted by America's experience as a nation; on the contrary, it had been confirmed

by material success. America was accustomed to being master
of its fate. History had not, as in Europe, been a prophet of
doom, but a friend. It had not entered American experience
that in this world a country often has to bow before forces
beyond its control; that it is circumscribed from without by
the power of another, and from within by the age-old routines
of the social structure; that defeat and not victory is the common human lot.

In 1906, H. G. Wells called America's mood one of optimistic fatalism. Only in America could that adjective be used
in conjunction with that noun. Only here did "fate" mean
the irresistible march towards ever new heights of well-being
and external power. Everything seemed possible to man in
this open society, open in space and in time—in its social
mobility bestriding a continent, in its confidence in the future.
The American present seemed always like an anticipated
future.

Now this mood is ebbing. It has not yet disappeared, it still
exists among the mass of the people, often diluted to mere
pleasure in the consumption of the products of industry. But
it no longer determines the thinking of the best minds. They
know that the Utopia has spent itself. Technology, which can
free man from every want by creating an undreamed-of living standard, has also given men the means of destroying
each other and the planet as well. Not even the status of a
major world power, which America has reached, can prevent
peace from resting on a balance of terror, when an opposing
Power in the East of Europe permitted America only a few
short years of supremacy. A fermenting mass of two billion
underprivileged people, in Asia, Africa, and Latin America,
threatens to upset the world's equilibrium altogether. Individual freedom has become ensnared in a vast maze of
organization.

Everywhere we find the same pattern: things are no longer
simple or easily controlled; they have become too complex,

too sophisticated, too powerful. History no longer appears in the guise of a friend, just as the ocean is no longer a shield. Now, for the first time, America has really entered human history, and must share the lot of all peoples: to sail against contrary winds, in which an "optimistic fatalism" can lead only to disaster.

It is easy enough to see that this mood of optimistic fatalism is still characteristic of most Americans, and indeed is hardly called in question. But the emphasis now is more on fatalism than on optimism, though the latter is still very evident as regards the well-being and happiness resulting from the consumption of goods. In the material sphere the idea of progress is intact. It could hardly be otherwise in a great nation of 180 million people who have achieved a standard of living unprecedented in human history, and who for the most part have not yet begun to doubt that in this way they have succeeded in the "pursuit of happiness" laid down in the Declaration of Independence, and that only quantitative advances are necessary.

As a result, the majority of Americans have entered the sixties in a confident, relaxed, self-satisfied mood, uninterested in adventure or excitement. They are primarily concerned with their private affairs, more than ever centered around their families. They are apolitical, trusting in the unbroken upward movement of industrial productivity, without fear of inflation or depression. Their only worry is whether peace can be preserved.

On this point there has reigned an unaccustomed sense of helplessness which—and this is truly paradoxical in the atomic age—has not appeared to affect the optimistic mood of the country. But the climate has markedly changed since the advent of a young and energetic President. The world situation is now viewed more realistically, in all its starkness, and at the same time the status quo is no longer regarded as so perfect that the incompleteness of American society cannot again

serve as a creative challenge. John F. Kennedy likes to speak
of the "unfinished business" of American society. In his inaugural address, on January 20, 1961, he said about America's
tasks: "All this will not be finished in the first hundred days,
nor will it be finished in the first thousand days, nor in the
life of this administration, nor even perhaps in our lifetime on
this planet. But let us begin." A year later, in January, 1962,
the President could thus define the changed atmosphere in
the country: "In 1961 the American people awakened as never
before to a sober realization of the perils that beset our nation.
Early complaints about the harsh sound of candor in the place
of complacency gave way to a grim determination to do whatever had to be done to preserve both peace and freedom."

In the pre-Kennedy era, George Kennan, speaking in
Washington, could say: "If you ask me—as a historian, let us
say—whether a country in the state this country is in today:
with no highly developed sense of national purpose, with the
overwhelming accent of life on personal comfort and amusement, with a dearth of public services and a surfeit of privately sold gadgetry . . . if you ask me whether such a country has, over the long run, a good chance of competing with
a purposeful, serious and disciplined society such as that of
the Soviet Union, I must say that the answer is 'no.'" Kennedy's electoral victory, in 1960, was perhaps the unconscious
answer of a majority—however meager—of the electorate to
this kind of criticism.

But there have also been other reactions to the status quo.
To begin with, there is the negative attitude of moral indif-
ference and "alienation," which is really the strongest refutation of Utopia, and, as such, troubles thoughtful observers.

The emergence of the affluent society in the fifties brought
with it certain moral developments which aroused doubts,
even in the consciousness of the mass of the people, about the
belief that a materially "good life" is automatically good spiritually and ethically. The heritage of a decade so successful in

a material sense is, nevertheless, a widespread moral uneasiness which cuts across the economic optimism. Much of what the moralists complain about may be ascribed to the diminishing religious force of Puritanism. America, unlike older civilizations, does not possess traditional standards which mark limits to conduct even in the absence of any "fear of the Lord"—which fear, so we are told, America has lost.

The television and radio scandals, the cases of corruption, the eight-fold increase in juvenile delinquency and two-fold increase in illegitimate births in ten years, the frequency of adultery, even in small towns, the development of the biggest narcotics market in the world, the devious paths trodden to make a "fast buck," where a dose of dishonesty does not really matter, and the unpuritanical tolerance shown all these phenomena, all raise some question as to whether the United States, after a short interlude as a World Power, is in a moral decline, and whether, sated, soft and debilitated as it is purported to be, it is therefore condemned to an inevitable and speedy loss of power, like other wealthy societies of history (particularly, perhaps, like Carthage).

In March, 1960, *Look* published the results of a survey conducted throughout the United States, showing that "a new American code of ethics" was evolving. This "code" is revealing. Whereas the traditional ethic condemns such things as perjury, deceit, fraud, forgery, theft, bribery and corruption, even though they escape detection thanks to some legal loophole, most Americans today hold them excusable on one condition: that they do not hurt anyone. *Look* analyzes the result: "A group morality appears to be replacing personal codes of ethics. That is, you no longer refrain from doing something because you couldn't live with yourself—you refrain from doing something because you couldn't live with your neighbors."

In other words, the "group" takes over the role of religion or ethics as the judge of what may or may not be done. The "group" means society. What is happening is that all values are subjected to a social relativism. Whatever insures success, as measured by the common denominator of the high standard of living, is justified, even if it is not ethical by former ethical standards—as long as it does not violate the law too flagrantly, in which case it is likely that the protectors of the law will call the violator to account anyway. And, even then (as in the case of Charles Van Doren, who became known throughout the world as the man who had cheated in a television quiz) the reaction is more one of pity than of puritanical condemnation—because it could, after all, have happened to any of us.

If this new "code of ethics" really exists, then society has dethroned all absolute, transcendental values. In other words, morality becomes a purely relative notion, unless inherited inhibitions remain which operate even when their metaphysical foundation has been lost.

As Dr. Robert E. Fitch, educator and author, sees the moral crisis, the moment one lets oneself be merged in society there is no such thing as humanity, let alone God or nature, there is only this particular society in which one lives, and over there another society, and ethics are "relative" to each individual social culture; the moment one yields to this philosophy, he concludes, one loses all objective standards.

How could such a situation develop out of the Utopian myth of the Promised Land? The answer lies in the distinctly American outlook which developed shortly after the first colonists had landed on the inhospitable though pleasing shores of the new continent.

The two centuries during which English communities grew up on the western side of the Atlantic were marked by a plethora of great philosophical systems in the Old World which the settlers had abandoned. The mentality developed by those who were later to be called Americans was immediately different. They were opposed to static systematizing, favorable to dynamic experience, prejudiced against the formation of a recognized intellectual elite, of an intellectual priesthood. Experience had priority over truth, and action had priority over the argument for action. The attitude that thus arose to the things of the mind was described by William James at the end of the last century. In America, he wrote, "the possession of truth, so far from being . . . an end in itself, is only a preliminary means toward other vital satisfactions."

In a book entitled *The Colonial Experience,* Daniel J. Boorstin points to the epistemological role of "self-evidence" in American thought, which was introduced in the Declaration of Independence as the source of basic rights. He regards this heeding of self-evidence, which is after all no less than a renunciation of metaphysical speculation, as the American "substitute for a philosophy or a philosophy for non-academic thinkers." This mental attitude comes out even more clearly in a passage describing the opinions of the founding generation: "If philosophy denied the innuendoes of experience," writes Boorstin, "the philosophy—not the experience—must be rejected. Therefore a man's mind was wholesome not when it possessed the most refined implements for dissection and ordering all knowledge, but when it was most sensitive to the unpredicted whispering of environment. It was less important that the mind be elegantly furnished than that it be open and unencumbered." Franklin declined learned disputes such as were favored by eighteenth-century Europe: "We are, I think, in the right road of improvement, because we are making experiments . . . The multitudes are more effectually set right by experience than kept from going wrong by reasoning with them." And Jefferson believed that "the opinions and beliefs of man depend not on their own will but follow involuntarily the evidence proposed to their minds."

The American Utopia was thus that astonishing thing: a dream, and at the same time, a reality; a reality nourished by a dream, a dream realized by experience. There was nothing abstract about it. It had to be so if the experiment of mastering an untamed continent was to succeed. Unlike Europe, America did not need the philosophical systems of Bacon, Descartes, Condorcet or Gibbon to perceive the straight line of progress in the web of history. Progress was a matter of daily experience. Or in other words, it was self-evident. Progress, to the beholder, arose out of the reality that met his eye. Boorstin quotes a minister, Andrew Burnaby, who visited Philadelphia in the middle of the eighteenth century: "Where only eight years before had been a wild and uncultivated desert, inhabited by nothing but ravenous beasts and a savage people, there was now a flourishing city." And this elicits the reflection: "Can the mind have a greater pleasure than in contemplating the rise and progress of cities and kingdoms? Than in perceiving a rich and opulent state arising out of a small settlement or colony? This pleasure everyone must feel who considers Pennsylvania." Progress was growth, expansion over regions full of promise. Utopia was only a step ahead of reality. Quite naturally practice prevailed over theory.

But as the distance between what was and what should be kept diminishing—the New World was becoming what it was intended to become, so men believed—the spiritual content of the Utopian myth diminished too. As it became interchangeable with reality, its metaphysical roots began to wither. The Founding Fathers and their followers, for all their belief in the self-evidence of things—that renunciation of intellectual speculation—were still swayed by convictions rooted in transcendental values. Indeed, "early American" idealism and its moral earnestness still survives among many of the older generation. But in the affluent society of the second part of the twentieth century, where Utopia and reality appear to coincide, society has become supreme, for it has attained all its goals or is on the point of attaining them. And as society has become the supreme measure of all things, a "socialization" of values has taken place which was already implicit in the original tendency to seek truth in the "whispering of environment." The final arbiters of individual action are the values of a society intent on enjoying its material abundance; not values external to society. And then empathy, the ability to put oneself in another's place, becomes the highest virtue.

The American Utopia, now apparently achieved, could become the greatest earthly approximation to perfection if its issue—this society—did not manifest such disquieting features. Could it be that the Utopian myth had miscarried after all, because the price of its achievement—the atrophying of its original metaphysical impulse—was too high? Many American social critics point to the following flaws under the bemusing surface of material abundance:

Freedom. Despite the formal democratic processes which have brought political autonomy to every citizen—with the exception of a racial minority—there is a growing sense of helplessness in the face of increasingly complex machinery of government led by a power elite that is often invisible. Self-government still exists on the local level, much more genuinely than in much of Europe, but the decisions taken by local units seem increasingly insignificant. Freedom of opinion, though never suppressed, is infringed on by the tendency of the powerful daily press to ignore unpopular voices which cast doubt upon the status quo. Such voices are consigned to weekly reviews with small circulations. The manipulations of advertising and the mass media bound up with it, such as television and movies, have aroused doubts as to whether the intellectual freedom of the individual is not a delusion.

Equality. Vertical social mobility, from bottom to top, has decreased, despite a growing classlessness in consumption. Distinctions of rank and status are congealing and becoming increasingly pursued. Equality is being undermined.

Mode of life. Urban decay has set in because the organic spatial relationship between work, life and recreation has been disrupted. The sphere of existence is split up into neglected business centers and suburban developments where local conformity is the order of the day. Between the two points lies a long, daily automobile drive on overcrowded streets where the individual caught in the traffic chaos feels like a lost speck, or a hot, jammed, train, bus or subway ride.

Economy. Complete satisfaction with the giant strides made in production is impaired by the disturbing contrast between the paucity of the public services and the abundance of private consumer goods.

Labor. Although the labor force, organized in huge unions, has become a power bloc on a par with capital and government (Big Business, Big Government, Big Labor), the individual worker's distaste for his unattractive position in a mechanized work process is increasing. Labor regulations have been enacted after bitter struggles, but labor has no part in decision-making. Here, again, there is a loss in organic relationships.

Education. Education is more highly prized as an instrument for molding citizens for democracy than as a means of fostering individual talent. As it has expanded on an enormous scale, so it has deteriorated in quality. The news of the Russian sputniks induced a severe trauma. The belief in America's technological superiority appears threatened.

Size and proportion. The population increase—thirty million in ten years—has stimulated the tendency inherent in highly-developed industries to overproduce. The departures from the ideal of freedom are the reverse side of the affluent society, with its drive toward quantitative greatness, towards the leveling of all human institutions. This loss of human proportions has placed irresponsible power in the hands of managers, manipulators, propagandists, and other intermediaries between the individual and a society that has become larger than life.

Here we have presented, in brief, some of the negative

aspects of the American society. *The following chapters will show that there exists so much capacity for self-redress, so many sources of strength in this as yet unfinished American society, that one surely need not despair about the future of this nation or of the West.* But it is necessary to emphasize the shattering of the Utopian myth—and the need for remedial action—to understand so strange a phenomenon as that of "alienation" in what is, *par excellence,* the optimistic society.

The individual can defend himself, if he so desires, against an over-powerful society, not by noisy revolt or by protest on behalf of social reform (what should he protest about anyway in the midst of abundance and protected by social security?) but by withdrawal, by standing apart, by becoming a stranger to society, silent, bored, apathetic, indifferent. That is precisely what is happening among large sectors of American youth, who have in consequence been called the "silent generation." Europe's "angry young men" reject certain specific conditions in their cultural environment; their American counterparts, far more numerous, protest mutely. The mute rejection is far more profound than the vociferous one, for it denies that society has any importance at all, that it is worth reforming.

Since American youth refuses to articulate its rejection clearly, since the materially accomplished Utopia of the adult world evidently leaves little more to be desired, it can only be assumed that the failures of society to which we have referred above have contributed to the impulse toward alienation.

The reality of that alienation, in any case, is indisputable: American youth tends at the present time to interpose an ever-lengthening moratorium, as it has been called, between childhood and adulthood, a drawn-out period of "disengagement" from the roles which it will eventually have to assume in adult society. Kenneth Keniston, a social scientist in his early thirties, maintains that the young man or young woman who enters adulthood today joyfully, and without hesitation, is the exception, not the rule. There is a separate "youth culture." While education has increasingly stressed the autonomy of childhood, industrial society has reduced the attractiveness of adult life. The humanization of childhood, Keniston maintains, is accompanied by a dehumanization of adulthood: hence the emergence of a "youth culture." To this "youth culture"—and we shall see it more clearly in the extreme case of the Beat generation—the young man withdraws from a system in which he obscurely senses something to be wrong. In a society which purports to be an earthly Utopia this is both puzzling and agonizing, and can hardly be ignored as a symptom.

The term "self-alienation" which Marx used in an economic context is used by American psychologists, like Erich Fromm, to express man's spiritual alienation from his own creative potentialities. Now the sociologists have begun to speak of the alienation of one part of society from the rest, the very part with which the future rests. Alienation presents itself as a way out when those positive values are lacking which nourish the will to reform and revolution. To the extent that this can be ascribed to the crisis of values in the West, to the upheaval effected by psychoanalysis, historical materialism and existentialism, America is only taking part in a process common to the West as a whole.

But there is one circumstance which—for the present at least—is peculiar to America, and represents perhaps the deepest source of alienation. It might also be a source of hope. Only in America does a causal relationship exist between alienation and abundance. It is in the form of an abundance of goods that the affluent society visibly expresses productive man's triumph over the forces of nature. But because this society has become so complex, mobile, restless and immense; because it seems to be directed by impersonal forces, the individual's feeling of helplessness is greater than ever before.

This may be a condition that is building up throughout the Western world; in America it is already a fact, and one answer to the harsh contrast between power and powerlessness is alienation. But it will not be the final answer. For never before has it entered into the experience of mankind that abundance should be the natural "human condition."

Just as economic theory has not yet caught up with the fact of abundance, rather than want, being the basic problem of the American economy, so "alienation" is only an indication that the heirs of the generation which achieved the great triumph over human poverty and want take prosperity for granted. That being so, they see no reason to strive toward it. Their energies have therefore been released for the pursuit of other things which they vaguely feel are lacking in this society. If there were no such spontaneous acceptance of different values, at least dimly perceived, there would be no reason to reject the social status quo. (Keniston calls this the "integrity of youth.") Alienation contains this hope, that in overcoming it, society will finally "humanize" abundance. For abundance is also a burden, however much that may contradict all our conventional beliefs. It is a burden because it releases moral and spiritual yearnings from the yoke of daily necessity, not merely for a small section of the population at the top of the social pyramid, but for almost everyone, and these unsatisfied yearnings, at least in youth, turn into cultural uneasiness.

But the silent generation has at last found a voice in the "Beatniks," and a very strange voice it is. Alienation has become for them another way of realizing Utopia, the anti-type of the Utopian communities of America's beginnings, and a more glaring contrast is difficult to imagine.

"When the barbarians appear on the frontiers of a civilization, it is a sign of a crisis in that civilization," writes Lawrence Lipton in *The Holy Barbarians,* the first monograph on the Beat generation. Since they come, he adds, not with the weapons of war but with the songs and images of peace, the crisis is of a spiritual order. The Beat generation is the Bohemian successor of the "lost generation" of the twenties and the Marxist avant-garde of the thirties, but though, like its predecessors, it represents rebellion against society, the rebellion is of an altogether different kind.

The Beat generation pushes self-alienation from present-day society to unheard-of extremes, just as that society indulges in an unheard-of superabundance. To that extent it is inconceivable outside the context of the affluent society, whose values it so furiously rejects.

In all the big cities, in Los Angeles, San Francisco, Chicago, New York, New Orleans, Seattle, hundreds of young nonconformists, mostly between the ages of eighteen and thirty, have banded together in the most radical repudiation of the society in which they were born. They come from different social levels, but more often from the middle class than from "below"; many of them have attended good universities, some have the experience of big business organizations behind them. They are not—or not typically—social failures.

The Beatniks do not rise against society. They reject it, break with it. They break with its economic system, with its ideology, which they call a "social lie," with its values, which they despise, in particular the nationalistic values of war (be it hot or cold) with its commercial civilization of success, which they call the "rat race," or *money*theism. It is not untrue to regard them as part of the pacifists and anti-capitalists of the nuclear age, but that does not cover their significance as a social symptom. Nor are they of the left, for they are altogether apolitical. They are the visible manifestation of social displacement; all that society displaces spiritually, metaphysically, is manifested in them. In the most literal sense, they have driven themselves out of society, and live in voluntary alienation like an ejected spiritual complex. They have not produced any really important works, but their existence is more significant than their creations.

Their relationship to society is something like the relationship of a monastic order to the world—except that this is an "order" whose adepts smoke marihuana, religiously reject prayer but whisper instead to the sound of the jazz canto, practice the broadest sexual and racial tolerance (as jazz musicians, Negroes are an indispensable element of these communities), celebrate the mysteries of sexual love as the antithesis of romantic love (one is "cool," like cool jazz), live in a "natural society," as Kenneth Rexroth puts it, held together by "an all-pervading Eros."

In a vocabulary unintelligible to the uninitiated, the Beatniks also call themselves "Hipsters," from "hip," which means something like "knowing," liberated from the intellectual deceits of society, seeing through them and therefore rejecting them. Their anti-type, their specific enemy, are the "squares"—the solid citizens—all the non-Beatniks, all who live within the "system," in other words, all Americans with the exception of a few thousand Beatniks. The Beatniks also call themselves "cats," because these unattached, promiscuous prowlers come nearest to the Beatniks' way of life.

Their deepest passive revolt against the consumer society resides in their attitude to property. They have been called—by the kindly-disposed—"Holy Barbarians," because they have chosen voluntary poverty after the manner of St. Francis. Consequently, they always live in slums; they accept work only in order to provide for their daily needs, but always temporary, casual work, mental or manual, and they give it up as soon as they have earned enough money—"bread"—to last them for a while. (This is what Sombart called the pre-capitalist "idea of sustenance," as opposed to the profit motive.) They do not want any work which would involve them again in the economic system, which they regard in the same way as the conscientious objector regards the military. They do not want any work which would be incompatible with wearing a beard and devoting their nights to jazz, sex, narcotic dreams, poetry and painting. Their philosophy is Zen Buddhism, which they prove *ad absurdum* with Socratic assertions combined with talmudic and scholastic concepts, as in the dialogue which Lipton taped—"Anyone want to be God?"—which ends with God becoming an atheist and therefore not existing any more . . .

What counterforces are there which operate against alienation in the affluent society?

That is, what spiritual and moral reserves does America possess? The people of the United States entered the present decade in a mood of doubt. On the one hand the United States was potentially the greatest nation on earth; on the other hand, its people were altogether unclear as to what to do with that greatness. Thoughtful Americans debated in private and in public whether the United States had lost its "national purpose." An historical cycle had closed, a period covering many decades of exhausting effort, including two world wars and a depression which had rocked the foundations of the economy. Before the new cycle could open, the great nation seemed to have slipped into a state of idle tranquillity, of complacency about its achievements, sheltered by the measureless power of the atom.

Those achievements were astonishing enough. Abundance was the normal condition of the society and poverty was dying out. Even though the Utopian myth had been shattered, if reality was measured by the original dream, then the battle with material want as the normal human condition had been won. The feeling therefore seemed justified that a cycle of decades, if not of centuries, had been completed.

The aim of the American experiment had been attained in the world of visible things. And that world had always attracted Americans more than the unseen world of values and ideas. Or, to put it better, the eighteenth-century idealism which characterized the settlers of the New World was never something abstract and independent of the visible world. The idea of progress, as we have seen, was not the product of a philosophical system but the daily accomplishment of the task of building the new society.

It would seem to follow that, in America, ideas transcendant to the social group cannot become creative if divorced from action. Only in fulfillment, in action, do ideas become a power. Action is the catalyst of the ideal. If action is replaced by complacent enjoyment of the fruits of action, the reserves of idealism fade. Then there is a danger—partly because they must remain unused—of their disappearing altogether. And if they disappear, how can America be true to itself?

For America, unlike other nations that have grown slowly, always has to prove itself anew in action. It cannot just be there. Its experiment in living must constantly improve if it is not to deteriorate. As a people, the Americans have a built-in mechanism—doubtless of Puritan origin—which prevents them from being cynics. It was not always possible for them, in the 1950's, to enjoy their prosperity without moral misgivings. Nowhere do people criticize their own system so constantly and so mercilessly as in the United States. Such criticism was rampant even at a time when the system appeared to have surpassed itself in procuring the welfare of the people at large. For the notion of perfection as something already achieved paralyzes American idealism. When deeds are denied it, because everything already seems done, then the idealism itself is called into question.

The two strongest elements in this idealism are the sociopolitical idealism which created the American State in the eighteenth century, and religious Puritanism. The latter, though its taboos have long become weakened, remains effective as a restless striving for improvement, a striving to do things well—efficiently—if they are to be done at all, a heritage of the Puritan notion of craftsmanship.

In the Preamble to the Constitution (the oldest living constitution of mankind) we find: "We the people of the United States, in order to . . . secure the blessings of liberty to ourselves and our posterity, do ordain and establish this Constitution for the United States of America." "To secure the blessings of freedom" had always been a dynamic process, not a settled condition. In the fifties, however, the unprecedented high level of prosperity seemed to be the realization of earthly perfection, and the securing of the blessings of liberty seemed to require no more effort or sacrifice. The Eisenhower years, with their mild climate of moderation, of the middle way, of carefree acceptance of the status quo, gave this mood the sanction of the Presidency, which must always be the specific center of direction of this pluralistic, centrifugal society, of this porous State. And no other impulses emanated from that center but those which encouraged people to regard the existing order as the best of all possible orders.

But a standstill, even accompanied by staggering feats of production, a standstill in the sense of an absence of great tasks, contradicts the law of America's being. America's reserves of idealism must ever again be challenged to achieve the unaccustomed or the impossible. They cannot feed on a metaphysic divorced from action; they need what Americans like to call "vision," but which is actually a very definite task imposed from above or by external circumstance.

The simplest, but also the most unsuitable pattern for this is the mobilization of forces required by war. In the two world wars and the Korean war, the American people started from scratch and achieved the extraordinary, both morally and materially. Franklin Delano Roosevelt, who knew his people very well, put the tasks demanded by the war effort at a maximum—for instance, a tremendous number of airplanes to be built in shortest possible order—because the harder the tasks, the stronger the appeal to the potential of idealism.

The same applies even more to the tasks of peacetime. The great social reforms of the New Deal in the thirties and the

Marshall Plan in the fifties, were peacetime endeavors nourished by moral sources of compassion.

But in the fifties there came a breathing space sanctioned from above, a repose in the perfect status quo of an affluent society protected by the balance of atomic terror.

Now, in the sixties, the United States has again entered an active era, which will renew its native faculties of idealism. It has recognized that its affluent society has to be made more meaningful if the grounds for alienation are to be eliminated. Despite the world rivalry in which it is engaged, it directs the energies of its inquiring spirit most passionately to the affairs of the society which the many waves of immigrants have built for themselves here on the North American continent. The American spirit is still at the service of the American "experiment."

Quantitatively, the circle is closed. There can no longer be any real "progress" in the ability to produce an abundance of goods for supermarkets, to distribute goods and services for private consumption across the broad continent, to promote even greater mobility, to invent still more electronic marvels, to consume still more of everything in still longer periods of idle leisure. It is in the qualitative sphere that the great new tasks lie ahead, because now, for the first time in history, people are beginning to be able to take the material things in life for granted.

In the period of unquestioning acceptance of abundance, many of America's moral resources fell into an uneasy desuetude. Now they seem to have been liberated. The qualitative improvement of society is being initiated once more. It is largely a silent counterrevolution directed against the "Jacobin revolution" which has held sway since the time of President Jackson, and represents a return to what may be called—in the antique sense of the word—the more aristocratic concepts of the Founding Fathers. Once again there is more government and less hearkening to those delphic oracles, the grass roots of plebiscitary democracy.

The goals toward which these qualitative tasks are directed have become visible. Many lines in this picture may confidently be expected to extend into the future. The American government still displays the peculiar characteristic which we might call its diffusion of power, but the Executive is battling more determinedly for wider powers which will make it more efficient in the contemporary world. The self-correcting devices of capitalism are being further expanded in order to adjust the economy to social needs and thus to humanize it; the rate of growth of the economy itself is becoming more dynamic and therefore more secure against cyclic crises.

Cars have shed their metallic sculptures, their tail fins and fussy chrome work, and their lines are again becoming sensible and functional. They have not ceased, however, to serve as secret dream symbols, as evidenced by the sports-car features that have found their way into the family cars.

Commercialism, and therefore the qualitative decline of television, continues to endanger that great mass medium. There are indications, however, that the regulatory power of the government will not much longer be restricted to the mere issuance of licenses, but that it will be used to establish, by means of persuasion, stricter cultural standards for the mighty electronic pictures.

Improved attitudes in the racial problem, that bitterest of America's internal problems, are slowly evolving, since the White House has given the necessary moral leadership. For the first time Negroes are approaching at least the outer periphery of the "power elite" whose citadels, the select clubs, are beginning, however hesitantly, to open their doors to colored members.

The new activism is apparent, also, in a field where quantity coincides, as it were, with quality: the immeasurable sphere of space, whose conquest must begin in the class room, and which only the two rival giant powers can hope to penetrate.

To Americans concerned with quality, concerned with humanizing a rich and sated social order, their society is still in the nature of tremendous, malleable raw material. Its very incompleteness constitutes its greatest hope. For it sets tasks without whose constant challenge America would cease to be America.

2.

The Permeable State

THE United States Government is curiously permeable in structure. It was born of the deepest distrust of the phenomenon of power. At its birth, it was in no position to act powerfully, and certainly not on a global scale, as history now obliges it to act. It is almost a mystery how the United States, without substantially altering the Constitution it adopted in the eighteenth century, has been able to play its part as the leader of a global coalition of anti-Communist States; how this great experiment in government, this politico-legal creation of the Founding Fathers, who dreaded equally the concentration of power at the top and the influence of radical majorities, has been able to survive under the conditions of the twentieth century.

The Founding Fathers established a federal government as the loose framework for what has come to be called the democratic process. The nation which was destined to spread across a continent flanked by two oceans had to be rendered capable of governing itself after the overthrow of British rule. But in their hostility to power, the settlers were also concerned with obstructing government as such, with splitting and neutralizing the exercise of power, by means of a multiplicity of safeguards. The government was set up as a permeable structure, as a transparent organism through which the energies of society would be able to flow freely and unimpeded. Thus, there came into being, as a result of the revolutionary Declaration of Independence, the system of checks and balances which has no parallel in anything that in Europe is called a government.

This experiment in government was fed by two deep, but contrary, streams of distrust. At first, in the revolt against the British Crown, the fear of dictatorial power was the stronger. But in only a few years, the fear of the contrary pole—of the power of radical democratic majorities—began to grip the ruling class. For in the century and a half of settlement of the East Coast, this class had become propertied and therefore conservative. Out of hostility to central power as such there arose the first principles of government of the new nation associated with the name of Jefferson. The swing of the pendulum against the almost anarchical character of this hostility led to the Constitution of 1787, which is most closely associated with Madison and the aristocratic Hamilton. But this swing of the pendulum only led to yet another kind of hostility to power— hostility to the power of the majority over the minorities, to which the propertied naturally belonged.

To forestall the tyranny of democratic majorities, political power was divided. Undivided power in government invited abuse; abuse, in the Puritan view, was inherent in corrupted human nature. Thus out of the American federal State there developed that "democratic process" which is as much concerned with impeding government as with making the country capable of government. Jefferson said that if offered the choice of "government without newspapers, or newspapers without a government," he would not hesitate a moment to prefer the latter. Government power was to be kept at an unavoidable minimum, jealously supervised by the majorities in the assemblies of the individual states. But the men of landed property and money, the conservative economic interests, the plantation owners with their Negro slaves, after the revolutionary impulse had achieved its goal of independence, were no longer much concerned with "popular rights," but were considerably more concerned with property rights and the need to protect them by firm guarantees. Thus there arose the system of checks and balances designed to safeguard minority interests, particularly property interests, from the "excesses of democracy."

It was the economic interests that most needed a centralized federal government, provided it never became strong enough to turn against them. At the price of neutralizing the government, sometimes to the very limit of its effectiveness, a governmental structure came into being which guaranteed the rights not only of the propertied minority, but of all minorities. Here, it seems, was another instance of what Hegel called "the stratagem of reason." By securing themselves against the leveling spirit of the unpropertied majority—as they called it— the propertied class created a loose political structure for the nation which was eventually to spread across the entire continent and develop into a dynamic, complex mass society, in which every minority—ethnic, racial, religious, social, or economic—could make its influence felt. As a result, thanks to the workings of the "democratic process," this permeable governmental structure was to facilitate the greatest internal reform of Western capitalism.

The fundamental concern of the Founding Fathers was to embody in the Constitution a system of government which would prevent both despotism and mass rule. The federal power was divided into three separate branches, the legislative, the executive, and the independent and powerful constitutional judiciary, whose duty it was to supervise both. In the legislative, reciprocal checks were provided by establishing a Senate to offset the House of Representatives—the representation of the "many." In the Senate, which had special powers in respect to foreign policy, the rich and well-born, according to Hamilton, would be able to curb the excesses and vagaries of electoral democracy. Such an aristocratic body, he contended, would subdue the stormy element of democracy.

The endlessly complex political power structure in America cannot be understood in isolation from this originally aristo-

cratic "counterweight." Of course the Senate is no longer re-
cruited from a particular class, though it is only since 1913
that its members have been directly elected. Nevertheless, it
remains an aristocratic organ of government in its political
style as a select group, an upper house whose members, secured by what is often a long chain of re-election, have seen
more than one President come and go.

In the *Federalist*, Madison could openly say that America's
political system should be based on what he termed the natural
inequality of man. The American Constitution is the exact
antithesis of the Jacobin Constitution. Its authors wanted at all
costs to avoid the establishment of popular rule by means of
parliamentary majorities. Therefore the President, the Chief
Executive, is not elected by Congress; he neither issues from
nor can he be overthrown by Congress (except by impeach-
ment, which can only be invoked on criminal rather than
political grounds and has never been successfully employed).
He is, in fact, elected by plebiscite (though formally by elec-
tors, in accordance with the original wishes of the authors of
the Constitution; so greatly did they fear the popular vote).
The President treats with the legislative almost as with a
foreign Power, an analogy that is especially apt when the
opposition party controls one, or even both Houses of Congress. That is a fate, incidentally, that hardly any President
has been spared during his term of office.

The third branch of government also enjoys the status of a
quasi-foreign power. At its head are the nine judges of the
Supreme Court, appointed for life by the President subject to
Senate approval. Each of the three branches of government
has a tendency to step into any power vacuum left by one of
the others. There have been times when the Supreme Court
has influenced the destinies of the country more strongly than
the President or Congress. Presidents, on the other hand, have
always been judged by the criterion of strength: whether they
were "strong" Presidents or not. Experience has shown that in

the long run no one can be over-powerful under this system
of checks and balances; but if one of the branches of government is weaker than it should be, an imbalance is immediately occasioned. This disturbance, in turn, is offset by new
power coalitions in this flexible system. That is how the
American Leviathan operates. Leviathan, not by reason of the
excessive power of the State (for that is precisely what the
State does not possess) but by reason of the sheer size and
differentiation of its mighty governmental machinery.

The bare outline of the governmental powers which hold
each other in check gives only an insufficient idea of the way
in which the will of society flows through this permeable
structure.

Whatever is absorbed from this flow is politics; in this way
the laws, decisions, actions, planning, which together constitute the government and administration of the country, are, as
it were, crystallized. That is how America is governed, if this
may be called government. But this "democratic process" has,
perhaps, a boundary, beyond which lies the real kernel of government action. The exclusion of undivided power from the
State has had the unlooked-for consequence that American
society has become the most power-conscious, indeed the most
avidly power-seeking society in the world. Power oscillates in
the immense apparatus that extends from coast to coast, and
every ambitious man has always been tempted, in the absence
of an hereditary aristocracy, to grasp at that ephemeral prize.
But power is seldom sought for its own sake; history shows
that power as such, in the sense of dominion over others, has
no particular attraction for Americans. Hence, too, power—in
the widest sense, and in its multifarious aspects, from political,
financial or military power to technological, religious or social
power—does not have a restrictive effect, as it has in Europe;
it does not restrict the freedom of others. It does so, of course,
in the sense that free competition may give an advantage to
one at the expense of another; but out of the power-saturated

atmosphere of this society there also develops its constant forward striving, its dynamic inability to stand still, its restlessness.

Power is often sought for the sake of the riches it can procure; that is why corruption and not dictatorship is the greater danger where politics is conducted as a profession. But today this danger is largely confined to the party "machines," themselves on the decline, which contend for the lucrative control of the big cities.

In the last few decades certain definite power shifts have taken place, but they have not crystallized to the point where one can say that this or that group, stratum, or class dominates the State. The growth of government operations has favored a concentration of power in the executive rather than in the Congress. A military build-up is unavoidable under present international conditions. The giant corporations are becoming increasingly powerful at the expense of the smaller enterprises and farmers. The mass media of the press, the radio and, especially, television have overtaken older institutions such as the universities, churches and clubs as factors of influence. The almost uninterrupted stream of commercial advertising which inundates the daily life of the nation, equipped as it is with psychoanalytic techniques and "motivation research," constitutes a source of influence of dubious merit. And yet none of this has really changed the fundamental character of this society, a character which also determines the political element: it is a fluid, open, pluralist society, splintered into countless power centers (for instance, fifty states), into ethnic minorities (everyone belongs to some minority in relation to the whole, from the old dominant Anglo-Saxon group to the Asians and Negroes) which all contend for their status, to keep it or to gain it, into rival pressure groups, individual social forces which try to move the gigantic Leviathan in the direction of this or that set of interests.

The Founding Fathers' fear of the mass rule of the majority has not been justified by events. America has become a mosaic of minorities. Not merely minorities in the usual sense of national groups (which have preserved themselves much better in the "melting pot" than was to be expected) but also in the sense of purely individual forces, representing no one but themselves, which work at the fabric of political power: lobbyists in Washington, industrial leaders, trade-union leaders (who have not long been sitting at the table of the mighty), chairmen of congressional committees with investigatory powers (which the late Senator McCarthy, though not unpunished, could abuse), the "veto groups" which, if they cannot make their own policies prevail, are nevertheless in a position to obstruct the policies of others (as for instance the Southern senators in the racial question)—all these are tiles in the great power mosaic. The two political parties are no exception to this rule; they too are composed in mosaic fashion, representing more or less loose coalitions of groups and not homogeneous political organisms.

American society could be as flexible and pluralistic as we have described it and still bear some resemblance to the older governmental structures of Europe were it held together by a strong professional civil service. But that too is lacking, and, despite the growing concentration of administrative power in Washington, it is doubtful that it will ever come into being. Although the spoils system—the apportionment of official posts to the victorious party of the moment—is on its way out on the administrative level simply for reasons of efficiency, at the highest echelons of the administration, including the greater part of the personnel of the government departments, the rule still holds that no one must own the government, least of all the civil servants. The American public service, including the civilian personnel of the Pentagon, comprises 2,400,000 persons, only a small percentage of whom can be compared with the permanent civil service in Europe. The barrier to a strong bureaucracy in the United States partly consists in this: a post filled by appointment carries only slight prestige with the public as compared with a post won in an electoral contest. It may be an exaggeration to say that a professional civil service is regarded as "unAmerican," but it is certainly not a distinctively American institution, as the strictly hierarchical bureaucracy, with its traditions of high self-esteem, is characteristic of Germany.

American officialdom is the exact anti-type of the mercantilist officialdom of continental Europe. In the United States it was not officials who built up the economy. The economy was there at the outset and itself became increasingly bureaucratized, developing giant organizations and creating in its wake a civil service to supervise, regulate and administer what would otherwise have become chaos. Even the internal development of the government agencies has been modeled on the economic bureaucracy. The privately owned railroads, the harbors, transportation, telephone, gas, the banks, the trusts, the labor unions, and finally the wave lengths and atomic energy have all had to be regulated. Thus there has arisen a comprehensive public service structure. The two world wars and the intervening economic depression of the thirties, with their attendant mobilizations, the New Deal and the Fair Deal, resulted in the further growth of administrative intervention in the life of the nation. The guarantee of social security, which is still quite heatedly referred to as a product of the Welfare State, is nevertheless today taken for granted, just like the guarantee of military security which the Government has to provide. American officialdom is the product of wars and crises, and in such emergencies it has had no difficulty in attracting the most competent personnel. Franklin D. Roosevelt's "Brain Trust" of the New Deal era, for instance, was notoriously a rallying point for talented intellectuals. But in normal times the pull of the dynamic industrial society is so strong that the problem of recruitment to the permanent

civil service has so far remained without solution. Is it perhaps a peculiarity of the structure of American society that
the nation can be really effective politically only under the
pressure of great emergencies? And can such a state of affairs
persist at all in the second half of the twentieth century? Let
us take a look at the internal mechanism of the government.

A senior political official in Washington has to proceed altogether differently from his opposite numbers in European
capitals with their venerable traditions. Here, one can see
most clearly what can be called the permeable nature of
American government.

More than two-thirds of the top personnel of the Federal
Government—the senior officials, from Secretaries to divisional
heads in the government departments, and the heads of the
many committees, agencies and technical agencies, which have
the status of small ministries, even if their chiefs are not in the
Cabinet—are political appointees. About 1,100 of these top
posts in the executive branch are occupied by persons appointed by reason of their party membership. For the most
part, these people have only temporarily left their private
professions, and, often, they have no political experience. At
first they have great difficulty in picking their way through
the endless maze of Washington politics. Often, indeed, they
do not succeed at all, and may even be worn out in this strife-
ridden arena before they have a chance to escape back to
private life. These are the people who direct the machinery of
government under the authority of the President and the
Cabinet, together with the four to five hundred senior professional civil servants who occupy the higher posts (particularly in the State Department, since amateurishness in foreign
relations is conspicuously out of place). They are, so to speak,
the Government, in the sense of the body which carries out
the day-to-day functions of administration and makes the
decisions on which they rest. As they work, so the American
Government works.

Government action has expanded enormously. The Federal Government in Washington, with its branches throughout the country, has become the biggest business in a land of big business. Although private industry has developed into gigantic concentrations of economic power, it is far outstripped by the Government. The Government employs some 2,400,000 civilians; the armed services number about as many members. Compared with this, the biggest private concern, the American Telephone and Telegraph Company, has 800,000 employees; General Motors has 600,000 employees; the three next biggest firms, General Electric, United States Steel and the Great Atlantic and Pacific Tea Company, employ between 200,000 and 300,000 persons each.

A whole series of departments and special agencies have larger staffs than most big businesses. The Post Office comes first with 540,000 employees and officials; then comes the Department of Defense, which includes the Army with 416,000 civilian employees, the Navy with 364,000, and the Air Force with 316,000. The Veterans Administration has a staff of 172,000, the Department of Agriculture 101,000, the Treasury Department 56,000, to cite a few figures illustrating the proportions of this Leviathan. There are sixty-five agencies equivalent in magnitude to government departments, and about 350 bureaus, either sections of departments or special agencies. These bureaus employ an average of some 1,800 persons each, with forty-five of them employing over 5,000. They lead a curiously autonomous existence. They are the checks, within the Executive, in the system of checks and balances. They display—or attempt to at least—a disconcerting independence of their superior officers or department head. They are the smallest, but certainly not the least influential concentrations of administrative power in the civil services of the government departments; at the same time they preserve the permeable quality of the Government for the benefit of the social forces which compete unceasingly for its control.

Since America does not possess a parliamentary government, since, on the contrary, the Constitution is determined
by the conflict, deliberately built into the government, between the legislative and executive powers, Congress cannot
be the personnel pool for the manning of the upper echelons
of the Executive. Because of the profound distrust of any
permanent power, professional civil servants, too, are virtually
excluded. Recruitment, therefore, has to come mainly from
extra-governmental spheres. The preference is for leading figures from the great industrial concerns and investment banks,
and from the law firms—"law factories"—closely related to
both.

The running of the Government is regarded as a form of
business management. The man who directs a private business
and the man who directs a political unit are both managers;
both have to administer multi-tiered organizations consisting
of people. Their functions would therefore seem to require
quite similar qualities. The political "manager," like his counterpart in business, has to direct his organized subordinates
with humanity, so that they cooperate spontaneously; this is a
wholly different concept from that of the chain of command
operating from the top, based on the authority of the State,
the reason of State or even a State mystique. The Government
as an independent power in relation to society, with its own
majesty, and striking fear into the heart of the individual—
such a phenomenon is unknown in America. Hence, the absence of title-seeking. The citizen does not take pride in a
strong Government; on the contrary, he makes government as
private a thing as possible, and therefore also as human a
thing as possible. Of course, he weakens it by the same token,
but intentionally so.

But when a business executive comes to Washington to take
over a department, a departmental section, a regulatory commission or one of the influential technical agencies, he soon
finds that life in a world power center is different from life

at the head of a business organization, however massive. Because the Government is essentially a loose power structure, constantly seeking to maintain its equilibrium by readjustments, the higher political official has to conduct a war of movement on many fronts if he is to hold his own and serve the interests of his agency.

The Brookings Institution, a Washington research organization, reported a few years ago on a round-table discussion among a group of high officials concerning the duties of the departmental civil service. Only a fraction of the working day of agency chiefs is taken up by administration in the strict sense of the word. Endless energy, nervous strain and time are expended on activities resulting from the deliberate division of power which we have described. Up to one-third of the day is often swallowed up by contacts with Congress. In private industry, there are boards of directors, but these are distant divinities who seldom bestir themselves, as compared with the merciless control exercised almost daily by the congressional committees as supervisors of the administration. Not only do these committees have control of the purse, like all parliaments, which they use according to prescription often down to the smallest detail, but they also have the right at any time to summon Cabinet members, department heads and bureau chiefs for hearings. A part of the service duties of high officials is to "deal with" Congress. It is one of the American paradoxes, arising out of what has been called America's capacity for ambivalence, that the division of power between the executive and legislative branches has led to this contrary situation: the supervisory rights of the legislative are used for uninterrupted interference. Congress has great power to paralyze the executive, and to prevent the use of this power a departmental official must have the diplomatic ability to "hit it off" with Congress. The same applies to professional public servants.

This is a far cry from the European tradition of the

politically neutral, permanent civil servant. In the native American tradition, the professional civil servant has a political responsibility; he has to defend the program of the existing administration before Congress and the public. Should this bring him into conflict with his conscience, the only alternative is resignation, not transfer to some politically colorless post. All this is part of the general picture. The United States Government is made up of men who have not pulled up their roots from the soil of a dynamic society, and are not expected to, for if they did, so it is believed, government service would have no attraction for really gifted men. A career official has said about this: "As a careerist, I am still a man of conscience. I reserve the right to have a conscience, to have my own beliefs and argue them in the proper places within the Government."

This very American position, originating in the right to resist any abuse of power by the State, laid down in the constitutions of the individual American states even before the French Revolution (for which they were a model), certainly suffered in the years of the anti-communist witch hunt led by the late Senator McCarthy. It seriously affected the morale of the career service and made it even more difficult to resolve a basic problem of this democracy, the recruitment of dedicated and skilled politicians and officials. But McCarthyism appears to have been in the nature of an infection which has now been virtually driven out of the body politic.

The splintering of power in the form of checks and balances cuts deep into the internal structure of the Government and obliges its leading personnel, from department heads to bureau directors, to engage in incessant interdepartmental, interagency negotiations. Thanks to the ever-present distrust of power, no agency is provided with an exclusive sphere of competence. It is enmeshed in an intricate system of reference from one agency to another, and in order to act at all, the agency heads have to negotiate compromises among themselves as well as with Congress. It has always been the American way to create a new agency when some new function has to be assumed by the Government rather than to assign that function to an existing agency, thereby strengthening it. The growth of the Executive has been compared to that of a farm: "A wing added to the house now, a new barn put up later, a shed built some other time, a silo at one stage, a corn crib at another, until it was spread over the landscape in a thoroughly confusing way." The 350-odd technical agencies and bureaus which make up the executive branch, either as parts of departments or as independent units, have developed in this disorderly, positively anarchic fashion. Each seeks to defend its mandate—which always has to be approved by Congress—and its administrative traditions against its hierarchic superiors, be these the department head or the White House itself. As a government lawyer has put it, "The department heads may be said to be faced with a chronic state of mutiny in their bureaus."

If this kind of friction in the chain of command was not planned, but has simply resulted from the development of the governmental machinery, the interagency rivalry, which forces high officials to "consult" with their colleagues in other units of the administration, was quite deliberately incorporated in the system. In that sense, America is the most liberal State in the world; just as truth, according to liberalism, emerges out of group discussion, so the closest approximation to the common good should emerge from the power conflicts between agencies which both cooperate and compete with one another. Basically it is the idea of competition transferred from the economic sphere to the sphere of government.

In the round-table discussion to which we have previously referred, one official declared: "Frequent explosions inside an administration can be very healthy. They are an essential ingredient of opinion-making in a democracy. They dramatize policy conflicts, spotlight areas of costly duplication of services. . . ." Competition within the Government, another says, makes the political officer more vigilant, more resourceful, more energetic. But: "Interagency rivalry certainly is one way to discover the public interest, but the rivalry ought to be resolved within the executive branch." And that is precisely what, for the most part, does not happen, as we shall indicate.

The most notorious interagency rivalry of recent times has been that between the Army, Navy and Air Force, involving bitter arguments on matters of strategy and budgeting. Many Americans believed that these fratricidal struggles conducted in full view of the public strengthened the armed services; in Europe such strife would be regarded as dangerously weakening them. The desired unification of the General Staff came to nothing; even in the atomic age the Napoleonic specter of the "man on horseback" has power to strike terror.

Under President Kennedy, however, Defense Secretary McNamara has been able to establish civilian control over the military apparatus in an unprecedented fashion; the aim is to distribute the armed forces on the basis of their common strategic missions and no longer according to the technologically superseded division into three or four services, for instance in the presentation of the budget. Thus, what may be described as a flanking maneuver of the civilian direction has removed the cause of an interservice rivalry.

Other "classical" agency conflicts have taken place between the Treasury and the Federal Reserve Board, the Agriculture Extension Service and the Soil Conservation Service, the Forest Service and the Grazing Service, the Department of Commerce and the Interstate Commerce Commission, the Department of Labor and the Department of Health, Education and Welfare, and, of course, among all those often powerful agencies which take part in shaping foreign policy. The deliberate fostering within the sphere of government of the competitive spirit that is naturally at home on the sports field or in the market place has inevitably led to strange alliances. They do not receive much publicity, but even if they did it is doubtful whether they would arouse much real indignation in the ordinary citizen. For they do not really contradict his view of government.

The bureaus—and many departments are actually agglomerations of bureaus—ally themselves with the interest groups which operate in their specific areas of competence, as well as with the congressional committees which cover the same area from a legislative point of view. Thus triangular alliances emerge which cut straight across the separation of powers. In the mobile composite of American politics, small concentrations of power are formed consisting of technical agencies, congressional committees and interest groups. Here we see "society"—internal power politics, trade union politics— clearly reaching into the most intimate cells of the machinery of government. Government power becomes fragmented, diffused. As Professor Harvey Mansfield describes it, interest groups attempt "to create a little government responsive to and dependent upon them. They strive to develop an island of power consisting of the pressure group membership which forms the clientele and supports its private government, a separate public agency dedicated to the service of that specific clientele, and a ring of outposts, agents, allies and dependents, reaching into the other centers of power—the White House, the relevant legislative committees and appropriation subcommittees of Congress, the cognate division of major executive departments, and the headquarters of the more inclusive pressure groups—that may impinge on its interests."

In this extraordinary system of piping power and influence, Congress is not a constant factor either. The legislative branch is permeable too, not so much because it is split into two parties, but because its real power, which contributes to the shaping of policy, lies in its approximately one hundred committees and subcommittees presided over by members of the majority party in accordance with the rule of seniority. These hundred chairmen and a small number of party leaders embody the power on Capitol Hill. They, as a matter of course —and successfully—seek to transform the supervisory rights of Congress into personal power for the House. They also have their own staffs, trained over the years—a kind of congressional bureaucracy employed in the committees—which alternately cooperates with the government civil service and works against it.

The details of the game of power politics in Washington depend more than anywhere else in the world on personalities. The centrifugal forces in the structure of the State make the art of government extraordinarily difficult. But they also give persons of exceptional talent exceptional opportunities. John Foster Dulles well knew that he directed the only department which possessed no "constituency," no pressure group. He sought, therefore, to secure a base of domestic power outside the department. This he found in the right wing of his party in the Senate, as long as it was strong. A government official certainly need not be the tool of interest groups. The dynamic nature of the society nearly always allows vast room for maneuvering. When General Omar Bradley was Chairman of the Veterans Administration, he refused in a particular instance to support the views of the veterans' organizations, which are among the most powerful pressure groups. He lost their confidence, which certainly made his position very difficult, but when he made certain recommendations to Congress before leaving his post, it became evident that he had allies there. A few days later, the President signed a bill based on those recommendations.

The Department of Agriculture is under pressure from farmers' organizations; but since there are rival farmers' groups, the department head can play them off against each other. The same applies to the numerous pressure groups in medicine; doctors can stir up considerable excitement when their own interests are involved, as the American Medical Association's fight against the Kennedy administration's program for medical care for the aged through social security has proved. But pressure groups can also fight each other. In many cities, physicians have banded together to demonstrate to Congress that doctors are not uniformly against the Government's program. According to Jacob Burckhardt, power in itself is evil, but fear can greatly diminish its malevolence. This may be a curious remedy, but the American Government has prescribed it for its servants.

The almost systematic fostering of insecurity in the leading political representative of a World Power has its doubtful side —it could hardly be otherwise. Here, perhaps, we have the key to the perplexity of nations which depend on Washington's decisions or are affected by them—and what country is not in this second half of the century?—perplexity about the lack of consistency in American policy, about its hesitations, vacillations, indecision, lack of consistent principle. The deliberate fragmentation of government power which preserves freedom demands a price, a kind of unfamiliarity with the nature of political decisions. Policy making consists of choosing between alternatives and therefore always contains the seed of failure. The inner security of the individual, required for decisions, the kind of security which cannot be taken away by the group, is not strengthened by the process of decision making as it has developed in America.

The basic pattern is the committee system. Government in America is carried on through the thicket of committees, in which officials or experts or intellectuals—there is an increasing tendency to call in intellectuals as consultants—are pitted against each other until the group has reached a consensus, which is then regarded as the right solution. In this way, so it is believed, the tragic element of failure, which belongs to politics as shade to light, can be bypassed. What it really means is that instead of a clear—and possibly, of course, wrong—decision, a compromise is reached which leaves out everything controversial. Henry Kissinger puts it this way: "The more fragmented our approach to policy, the more difficult it becomes to act more consistently and purposefully. The typical pattern of our government process is therefore endless debate about whether a given set of circumstances is in fact a problem, until a crisis removes all doubts but also the possibility of effective action. The committee system, which is an alternative attempt to reduce the inward insecurity of our top personnel, leads to the paradoxical consequence of institutionalizing it."

The committee system is derived on the one hand from the separation of powers (which we have described) and on the other hand from the philosophy of pragmatic liberalism which permeates this very heterogeneous society for its good, but at the same time makes political action on the basis of new ideas very difficult. Not that American society, or the American Government, is not open to such ideas; it is more open to them than any other nation. But the system as a whole does not favor the speedy translation of these ideas into decisions, and actions based on such decisions. Hence, the very apparent inclination of the great American nation for the status quo. If political truth is thought to emerge from group consensus, and if such consensus can be reached only by exhausting debates in interdepartmental or technical committees, then the prospect of bold and original ideas (however plentiful they may be) surviving this filtering process is limited. (An anonymous wit invented this absurd image: a camel is a horse designed by a committee.)

Once a consensus has been reached on some concept of diplomacy or strategy, it acquires a tremendous *vis inertiae*. Humanly, it is very understandable that one should be reluctant to begin the cumbrous, time-consuming, nerve-wracking process all over again. This is one of the causes of what looks like rigidity. It is not rigidity in the sense of a characteristic trait, but an almost functional incapacity of the government mechanism to change course rapidly.

Nothing, probably, will be of greater significance for the history of the American Government in the present decade than the struggle to strengthen the Executive in relation to Congress. President Kennedy's requests for enlarged authority for the planning of foreign aid, for tariff negotiations, for directing the economy to prevent recessions, for instituting "qualitative" social improvements in the fields of education, urban renewal and the conservation and development of natural resources, all have the same aim: to make the helm of State more flexible in the hands of the Executive. Crises in foreign policy must be anticipated. America must stop being taken by surprise by situations for which it is unprepared and having to deal with them with the inadequate means inherited from the experience of the preceding crisis. This readjustment is what Walt W. Rostow, one of the intellectual "insiders," calls the new "national style" which the United States needs in order to survive in the global struggle. President Kennedy's most startling experience upon entering the White House was what he privately termed the unfortunate diffusion of power even in the highest office.

Before we ask how foreign policy can then be conducted in this country, we must mention certain specimens of the American flora which round out the picture of the social arena.

Some of these specimens are so uniquely American in origin that their names have passed unchanged into the European languages: for instance, "pressure groups" or "lobbies." Philologists have established that prior to 1832 the word "lobby" had been used only to designate a particular area inside the British House of Commons. In 1832, it was used for the first time to describe the totality of those who had settled, as it were, in the lobbies of Congress for the purpose of buttonholing senators and representatives and influencing legislation in one direction or another. In 1946, the word passed into official language in the Regulation of Lobbying Act, which brought to a close a century and a half of unrestrained activity in the antechambers of Congress. America had become the only country in the world to legalize the professional influencer of legislators and by the same token to subject him to public supervision.

In the thirties, the term "pressure group" slipped out of the sociology seminars into everyday language. At first it remained charged with polemical overtones, since it was mostly applied by leftist social criticism to the political influence of capital. Now, however, the term has no political connotation. It designates a socio-political reality which operates in this mobile society as a fact of nature. Pressure groups and their tools, the lobbyists, are regarded as a part of the legislative process; the play of social forces thus presses incessantly upon the Government. This often rather obscure sphere of activity has been somewhat clarified since the 1946 Act required that lobbyists be registered and their accounts inspected. Congress has conducted six comprehensive investigations of particular lobbies, showing its increasing sensitiveness to charges that it is subject to influence or even that it is venal. The moral issue is confused. But in general the rule is, as a senator from Missouri candidly put it: "A lobbyist is anyone who opposes legislation I want. A patriot is anyone who supports me."

Here again we find the principle of the loose framework. The enormous number of individual interests in this highly industrialized society are given free rein, even though the rules of the game are laid down by law. Just like opinions or power complexes in other fields, they are supposed to neutralize each other. If they all got what they wanted, however honorable their motives, Uncle Sam would go broke, as Senator Douglas put it. Senator Dougles estimated in 1950 that there were about four thousand national organizations in the United States with memberships totalling at least eighty million, each of which was actually or potentially a pressure group. They range from small groups—a few citizens, for instance, who want to prevent a construction project—to the powerful alliances of industrial and trade associations, trade unions, farmer associations, etc. Among such powerful groups are the Veterans of Foreign Wars, the oil, insurance and electricity corporations, and, at the same time, Bible societies, abstinence societies, brewery societies, atomic scientists, representatives of countries which receive foreign aid, and even a German lobby, which contends, in vain, for the return of impounded private assets.

The lobbyists do not only put pressure on the legislators, they also assist them. In contrast with parliamentary democracies, the American Government does not have the right to introduce legislation. Of course a committee member can always be found who will submit to Congress a bill that has been drafted by the Administration, but a great number of bills are drafted right outside the governmental sphere. That is where the lobbyist has become indispensable. He provides not only cocktail parties and dinner invitations, election funds and votes, but also data pertinent to legislation, information on the needs of a particular electoral district, statistical material, and objective viewpoints, as well as the naturally more frequent special viewpoints. This is not considered reprehensible, for out of these competing special viewpoints, laws are born. This is another instance of the way in which the pattern of the market place dominates American structures.

The first amendment to the United States Constitution, dated December 15, 1791, made the right to petition the government for a redress of grievances one of the fundamental rights of the citizen. Lobbying is regarded as the modern equivalent of the petition, which is why any attempt to interfere with the lobbies is met with the indignant protest of interest groups who maintain that such interference is unconstitutional. Attempts to exert influence in the antechambers of the legislature have never, in fact, been prohibited as such; the only thing that has been done is to hold them in check by touching their nerve center, money, since they now have to account for their funds. Money is not always the lobbies' aim, but it is always their means, without which they cannot operate. And money is more subtly used in the lobbying process than in the more old-fashioned forms of bribery and corruption.

Since the lobbyist has become a legally recognized power, his activity has received the stamp of respectability and lost the aura of secrecy and disrepute that formerly surrounded it. Now that all lobbyists have to register their own names and the names of their employers with the Clerk of the House and the Secretary of the Senate, and report on all monies received and expended above a basic minimum, the clarity, at least of numbers, has penetrated the murky tangle of conflicting interests and motives in which the lobbyists conduct their often fascinating battles. There were six times as many registered lobbyists in Washington in 1951 as members of Congress—over three thousand of them. Their salaries range from that of a company chairman to zero—as in the case of Michael P. Egan of Warrensville, registered as a philosopher and philosophical consultant, who carries lobbying to the extreme of opposing all special interests with his aim being to influence the legislators for what he calls the common good of the citizens of the United States (about which there is frequently little enough concern among his colleagues in the profession).

Methods of the utmost refinement are used to put the pressure of "public opinion" on legislators. Public opinion of this kind is often not only aroused by lobbies but actually synthetically created by them, with the lobbies representing themselves as the voice of a public opinion which they first manufacture. That is what happened, for instance, in the feud between the railroads and the trucking industry, in which powerful lobbies were involved. This is obviously a case where freedom can endanger itself.

The individual lobbies, like the organizations they represent, are oligarchically constituted. The few decide, even where the membership goes into the millions. Distant wires are pulled, mostly invisibly, by officials of the lobbies. Lobbying begins with the grass-roots, in the smallest units of the electoral district, which suddenly begin to deluge their representatives in Congress with telegrams, letters and every kind of message about some particular matter, such as Egyptian cotton or frozen fish from Iceland (the sponsors are against imports). That is the wave of public opinion on whose crest the lobbyist rides.

There are other ways too of manufacturing public opinion, through the press, advertising, films, and other forms of propaganda. They are very expensive; some lobbies have a yearly expenditure of millions of dollars.

The lobbies have long ceased to represent only the interests of big business. "Big labor" and "big agriculture" are also represented. Then there are the much noisier and often very combative groups, such as the American Legion and the Veterans of Foreign Wars, which concern themselves with safeguarding the "purity" of patriotic ideals and morality against "radical" social trends. Certain women's organizations have a similar aim, for instance, the Daughters of the American Revolution, who deserve mention simply because of their disquietingly antiquated character. On the other hand, there are groups such as the NAACP, which seeks to promote the integration of the colored citizens in a white society. There is an extraordinary jumble of economic power and moral, idealistic forces. For almost a quarter of a century, up until 1933, a wealthy abstinence lobby imposed prohibition on the country, until a counter-lobby finally succeeded in breaking the anti-alcoholic spell of the legislators. No lobby without counter-lobby; in this way even this perplexing institution is integrated in the "democratic process."

What, then, are the buttresses of this governmental process, without which the country as a whole would not be in a position to function at all? Are they the political parties?

The parties too, as America has developed them, are unique; and most unique—if such a superlative is permissible —are the great party conventions held every four years to nominate a candidate for the presidency. They are such oddities in the sphere of political organization that observers have been able to describe them only in terms of nonpolitical phenomena. James Bryce, for instance, compared them in his *American Commonwealth,* written over sixty years ago, to a medieval pilgrimage or the mustering of a great army. Others, less respectfully, have called them a modern form of tribal rite, a kind of war dance at which the chief is chosen and the victory mood kindled. And yet these conventions reveal most clearly the essence of both great parties.

They are giant mechanisms, innocent of any dogmatic philosophy, whose highest aim is to conquer the highest executive office, the presidency. They have become the machinery for selecting the potential incumbent. In their internal organization, however, they are more like a loose alliance of democratic feudal lords than strictly unified bodies. Local power agglomerations within the individual states, conservative forces and forces intent upon change, ensure that the parties are built on the pattern of the loose coalition that is so characteristic of America. Both parties have their conservative and liberal wings, and as often as not the like-minded wings in both parties act together against the rest (as in the classic alliance of archconservative Republicans and Southern Democrats). But here again, the American hostility to political power has prevented the conservatives and the liberals of the country from merging into two mighty opposing blocs.

In the nominating conventions, both parties appear as national parties, whereas normally the ordinary citizen sees them only in the context of a thousand single battles waged far and wide across the American continent. (There is no compulsory voting discipline in Congress, with the result that the party often appears as an appendage to the person rather than the reverse.) But what an unbelievably confusing picture the party conventions present to the bewildered observer! First, there is the great carnival atmosphere that is otherwise absent from Protestant American life. Here it is, with its brightly colored costumes, its clowning, its fanfares, its exuberance, very much the kind of thing one finds at particular times of the year in parts of Catholic Europe, except that here the motive is political. When lovely women pin ribbons across their chests with slogans favoring their candidate, when hundreds of prettily dressed teenagers put their youthful charm to work for this or that politician, when bare-shouldered girl acrobats form a human swing for their candidate in order to demonstrate the "swing" in favor of that candidate, then the two carnival worlds seem to meet.

Then there is the performance going on for days in plenary, with a cast of some twenty thousand persons, a party rally apparently little different from party rallies of other democratic nations. But most of the time what goes on there, under the glaring arc lights, has absolutely nothing to do with the purpose of the gathering. The real work is done elsewhere. Committees consisting altogether of not more than 100 party leaders work all through the night to secure agreement on the party program, which already anticipates the choice of the candidate. The ideological unity of the party has to be hewn out anew at each convention. It is not a fixed quantity. In fact, the farther one gets from the superficialities of the convention, the nearer one can approach the decisive power maneuvering which takes place in the intimacy of hotel rooms or caucus chambers, where delegations engage in secret consultations.

While the political carnival proceeds in full swing in the hot streets of the big city—conventions always take place at the height of the summer—the real game unfolds behind the towering walls of the skyscraper hotels.

The variations of power are endless. All kinds of things happen before the decisive choice is narrowed down to the few who have survived the process of elimination. The party delegations, representing the fifty states of the Union, their different voting strengths based on the size of their respective states, conduct themselves at first like independent States at an international conference. They use their ballots as coin for offices or for "planks" in the party platform. They are anxious to conclude satisfactory agreements with the potential future occupant of the highest office. But their own power is fluid, dependent upon whether the rival candidates in their effort to secure a majority still need them, or perhaps suddenly no longer need them. Nowhere can power fade so rapidly as at an American party convention.

The unadorned kernel of the convention—if the nomination is really a fighting issue and not a foregone conclusion—comes into full view when one considers the types of power which compete there. There is the personal prestige of elder statesmen, as enjoyed by Mrs. Roosevelt and former presidents Truman and Eisenhower. There is the power over future offices ascribed to the candidates believed capable of winning. There is the power over present offices in the sense that a politician who does not want to, or cannot, be a candidate still has influence over many delegations, in other words, a transferable power which he can bestow upon a claimant—the power of the key position, of the kingmaker. Finally there are the "favorite sons" of individual states, proposed by their delegations in any event and then, because they cannot win the nomination, withdrawing in favor of another; here voting power is contributed in the hope that such dedication will pay off later. Harold Stassen, for instance, built his transitory career in the Eisenhower administration on such a withdrawal.

Out of this conflict between different kinds and different holders of power there finally emerges a candidate and his running mate. It is a turbulent process, and the compelling question arises as to whether a great country has to use such means to find the men to govern it. Are there not more dignified and also more reasonable means? The answer is that no better procedure has yet been found for America as it is, with all its unfinished business, all its tensions and contradictions. So far no other way has been conceived in which the necessary adjustments and accommodations can be made within the same party without the piling up of social and racial dynamite—no other way than this quite open race for power. Victory is then fair, like the victory of the swiftest horse.

The looseness and elasticity of the American political system acts as a shock-absorber in serious conflicts. Thanks to it, the profound social upheavals of the last decades—the self-corrective action of capitalism, the taming first of capital, then of organized labor, racial integration by judicial decision—have taken place without political institutions having to be changed, without the incessant revolutions in the social sphere developing into political revolutions. The very conservative character of the system of separation of powers has not prevented change, only slowed it down and canalized it.

Strife pumps the blood through the arteries of this political organism, but what happens when strife ceases? Will the organism not become anemic? Can it remain fully competent when the will to fight slackens at every hand, when "moderation," the "middle way," becomes the watchword? Too much strife can destroy this singular form of government, but too little strife can be paralyzing too. This danger is endemic in the American system. For the past twenty years America has not had a decisive majority—Roosevelt lost it in Congress in

1938. Decisive majorities result from strife between the parties. The clearer the issues and the more passionate the debate, the greater the prospect that finally one party, for a time, will dominate the country and the centrifugal loci of power will be held together. But if the political climate becomes more temperate, as it has since the end of the last world war, if the "moderates" determine election results (there has been talk of the "revolt of the moderates" of the fifties) then party diffrences become more blurred than ever and neither Democrats nor Republicans can achieve a lasting, as opposed to merely a flash-in-the-pan, majority.

The result is that the party link between Congress and the Administration is often broken. Two different parties can rule at either end of Pennsylvania Avenue, on Capitol Hill and in the White House, each of the opposing forces elected by a majority of the moderates of the country. That the legislative and executive powers should normally be in the hands of contending parties—this is a separation of powers which goes even farther than Alexander Hamilton's conception of government founded on the principle of power to balance power.

When Wilson lost his majority in Congress in 1918, it became clear how disastrous such a situation, however temporary, could be for foreign policy. Although a farseeing majority in the Senate had decided in favor of American accession to the League of Nations, the decision was ineffective because it lacked the necessary two-thirds vote. Internal political pressures had triumphed, and they will triumph with increasing frequency in the conduct of foreign affairs, once the Chief Executive has lost his influence over the majority in Congress.

This state of checkmate between the powers of government is a permanent threat in a permeable State. When America's political system was developed, the protective ocean lay between what was later to be the United States and the rest of the world. To have spoken then of the primacy of foreign

policy would have been absurd. But the strategical revolution
of the atomic and rocket age has depreciated all protective
ocean frontiers. At the shortest notice, the North American
continent can become the object of a surprise attack. To survive, America has had to accept the painfully Prussian concept
of the primacy of foreign policy. But how does this concept
square with a political order which is an ordered disorder,
designed to make government as hard as possible? How can
it result in anything but indecision, hesitation, drift, obscurity?
That is the gravest problem confronting the United States as
a World Power in contest with other world powers.

Something needs to be said about the solution which America is in the process of finding for the vital problem of how to
become capable of action in the sphere of foreign policy. The
textbooks say nothing about it. The problem of American
competence as a World Power has emerged through a process
known to biology as osmosis. One dictionary defines osmosis
as a tendency to "percolation and intermixture of fluids separated by porous septa." The egalitarian American society is
studded with the most varied elites. These elites are "fluid" in
that they have no institutional demarcations. They are simply
there thanks to their sociological specific weight. Some of
these elites, by a process of osmosis, have coalesced into what
C. Wright Mills has termed the "power elite." This power
elite rules America in respect to formation of foreign policy.
It has taken over the invisible helm where the decisions are
made which determine the crucial issues of peace and war.

The formation of a firm center of action in the loose
American structure of checks and balances, in the power-
splintering democratic process, began about the time Roosevelt was preparing the United States for its entry into the
Second World War. It coincided with America's assumption
of its irreversible role as a World Power. The two developments interlock. What it means is that where foreign policy
becomes vital, it is taken out of the "democratic process."

Foreign policy ceases to be conducted as politics in general is still conducted in America. Yet something of the pluralism of forces neutralizing each other has penetrated even the action core of the power elite.

This became apparent, with world-wide repercussions, in the incident of May 1, 1960, when a United States reconnaissance plane was shot down over the Soviet Union. Each of the key agencies in Washington involved in the matter—the State Department, the Defense Department, the Central Intelligence Agency, the Space Agency and the White House—had acted more or less independently of the others. The result was initially diffused decisions authorizing the spy flight on the eve of an international conference, and vacillating handling of the diplomatic situation following the unexpected results of this flight. Never could such an unprecedented situation have arisen, in which the Paris Summit Conference foundered, had there existed any firm, central, policy direction. The incident is an example of the kind of obstruction which America has now to eliminate in order to be in a position to act as a World Power.

The American power elite is not a planned element of government. It is, as it were, the spontaneously generated response to the challenge of America's emergence as one of the two super-powers. (Here we see how apt is the analogy with osmosis.) But it has naturally crystallized around existing institutions. It has constituted itself, logically, at the top and is assembled around the presidency. But the way it has done so is very different from the way such problems have been resolved in the past in Europe. Here, we do not find an authoritarian or totalitarian head of State creating his tools from a strong bureaucracy or a powerful party apparatus. The American power elite is not the tool of the President who is chosen by plebiscitary process; rather, the reverse may be the case.

The United States presidency has been called an "impossible office." The burdens of the office have become superhuman. The President is a constitutional monarch for the duration, and at the same time the head of his own administration. Conceived of in the Constitution as a kind of paterfamilias of a deliberately weakened federal State, he has since become the leader of a global coalition of anti-Communist nations of East and West, the custodian of the demonic forces of the hydrogen bomb, and the administrator of a dynamic economy which he has continually to steer clear of the crises to which it is inherently prone. Despite all these responsibilities, not even the President has been provided with undivided power under this system of checks and balances. There is no strictly organized chain of command. The President tries to control the autonomy-minded departments and technical agencies through his Cabinet, but that often means setting a thief to catch a thief. That is why the White House, which up to the end of the nineteenth century managed with a diminutive staff of advisors, has been developed by successive Presidents into an executive organ of government, which daily and systematically concerns itself with the work of all branches of the administration. The aim is to unify and rationalize the operation of government as a whole. The White House now has a staff of some thirteen hundred officials. The Cabinet, which has no constitutional status, has become a permanent organ of coordination. The National Security Council has assumed the role of a super-cabinet; here an inner circle of the Cabinet consults with the Chiefs of Staff and the head of the Central Intelligence Agency regularly, and in all times of grave emergency. This is the actual foreign policy directive body of the United States, even if the final decision lies with the President alone.

It will never be possible to bureaucratize the office of President of the United States so that it will function evenly, regardless of its elected incumbents. It is basically a romantic office, as Arthur M. Schlesinger expresses it in his biography of President Franklin D. Roosevelt: "Implanted within [the President] there must be an image, not necessarily—or even desirably—explicit or conscious, but profoundly rich, plastic and capacious, of the kind of America he wants, of the vision of the American promise he is dedicated to realize, of the direction in which he believes the world is moving. . . . This vision of the future . . . provides his life with its magnetic orientation."

As though so much mystical confidence in the one individual whom the people's will raises to the throne every four years must be atoned for, the wings of his power have again been clipped. He is responsible for foreign policy, but he must not make it alone. As De Tocqueville wrote in 1835, the federal Constitution entrusts the permanent direction of the external interests of the nation to the President *and to the Senate*. Congress has the right to reject treaties, to approve or deny expense budgets without which diplomacy cannot function in a system of world-wide alliances, to prevent the appointment of ambassadors, and, alone, to make that most important of all decisions, the declaration of war. Were Congress still to use the substance of its power over peace or war, then the solution of competence through a power elite would be thwarted. In reality, however, the lawmakers of both parties have abdicated their right in this respect. The spirit of moderation which characterized America in the fifties facilitated a suprapartisan renunciation by the legislative—apart from occasional obstruction—of the powers in matters of foreign policy which it constitutionally shares with the President.

In issues of life and death, the legislative looks on, half-paralyzed, at what the executive does. The opposition, and indeed the Senate as a whole, no longer has any part in foreign policy decisions. This could not have been more clearly evidenced than in the resolutions concerning Formosa and the Far East, in which the Senate gave the Administration what was in effect a blank check for the decision to go to war, at a time when the Administration had lost its majority in the legislature. President Truman entered the Korean war without Senate approval; President Eisenhower consulted the National Security Council, not the constitutionally appropriate organ—the Senate—when he sent troops to Lebanon. Fifty treaties of alliance have, in any case, undermined the Senate's right to participate in such decisions.

This situation is often blamed on Washington's conformist attitude. But should not deeper causes be sought? Perhaps what is really happening is an unavoidable correction of democracy of a distinctively American order. De Tocqueville was dubious, one hundred and fifty years ago, about the degree of wisdom that the American democracy would show in the conduct of the country's foreign policy. Perhaps that wisdom lies in this: the democratic process has been set aside in the sphere of crucial decision-making, and this sphere has been silently taken over by an elite group.

The formation of a power elite at the seat of government, which, as it were, bypasses the democratic process, began around 1939. Roosevelt's New Deal had given the executive branch so much centralized power that the groups whose influence was decisive in society, because of their wealth, no longer wanted to leave the executive to itself. Since the Civil War they had left the manning of government to professional politicians whom they sought—often successfully—to control from without. But then began the process of osmosis, first between the economic and political leaders—both regarding themselves as managers in relation to their duties—and then, with the Second World War, including the military. The rise of the high officer class to the innermost circle of power is a completely new development in America (a symptom, perhaps, of Prussianization).

The concept of a power elite was coined by C. Wright Mills in his book of that title, published in 1956; since then it has passed almost uncontested into the working language of political sociology. Other social scientists had, of course, recognized the situation of fact, but Mills subjected it to systematic investigation. Since he violates a great many democratic taboos, he is not exactly a standard authority in civics. But he was recognized in university circles and taught at Columbia University in New York, until his death early in 1962. His central thesis is as follows: "There is no longer, on the one hand, an economy, and, on the other hand, a political order containing a military establishment unimportant to politics and to money-making. There is a political economy linked, in a thousand ways, with military institutions and decisions . . . If there is government intervention in the corporate economy, so is there corporate intervention in the governmental process. In the structural sense, this triangle of power is the source of the interlocking directorate that is most important for the historical structure of the present."

The high military, the heads of the great corporations and the politicians at the seat of government have coalesced because they have discovered that their interests coincide structurally. This is no conspiracy; the power elite has become the point of intersection for developments in the three fields of government, industry, and defense, and that is precisely why it is not a "ruling class" in the Marxist sense. (The rather irrational aversion of business to President Kennedy is evidence of this point).

Even in the central directorate there remains something of the loose coalition that is characteristic of American life. The three elites have united, but they are not identical. Their interests agree, but this agreement is primarily a common front, against an external danger, brought about by the primacy of foreign policy. The system, so it has been maintained, required a foe; in this point it may in the future prove vulnerable. It came into being by a very American, that is, a very dynamic, process. The elites poured into the vacuum which the traditional democratic methods of handling foreign policy decisions had been unable to fill.

The emergence of a power elite had no connection with the tendencies of either of the political parties. The process began under a Democratic President, was strengthened under a Republican President and confirmed by the new Democratic President. The presence of a power elite is the real reason for President Kennedy's appointment of so many Republicans to the highest posts in his administration. The parties can take over from one another, as they did in 1952, and the incumbents of the highest executive posts change accordingly. But what is more important is that they all come from the same circles. The problem of America's competence in the field of foreign policy has been partially resolved in mid-century because the leading industrial managers have profited from the increased powers of the State. These industrialists, who are neither professional politicians nor professional civil servants, but political outsiders, fill many of the key posts in the government.

One condition for the emergence of the power elite was the expansion of government power; a second condition was the concentration of economic power in the hands of a few hundred companies closely linked with the government through defense contracts arising out of a defense budget of some fifty billion dollars. A third condition is the state of permanent mobilization in which the two super-powers find themselves as a result of the cold war and the destructive new weapons technology. Important foreign policy decisions are no longer taken without consultation with the military. The hierarchy of some five hundred giant concerns, headed by industrial managers and the government hierarchy, headed by industrialists temporarily turned political leaders—these have crystallized as an action cell around the elected President, the only "democratic" figure in this elite. That is the strong framework of power which makes America competent to act, however chaotic may be the situation on the middle levels of decision, where pressure groups, parties, commissions, and committees, as well as hundreds of technical agencies, jostle for position. Mills contemptuously calls these middle levels the semi-organized congestion; but it is hard to see how the endlessly variegated American society could govern itself freely in any other way, at least where the issue is not peace or war.

The top decisions in Washington are taken by a group of some fifty men, comprising the President, the Vice-President, the Cabinet members, the directors of the principal technical agencies, the Chiefs of Staff, the head of the Central Intelligence Agency, and members of the White House staff. Only a few of these are professionals in government, party politicians or officials; most of them come from other fields, and many—many more, at any rate, than in any European State—from the world of finance and business. Even though Kennedy has filled many important posts from the economic sector of the power elite, it is quite evident that he does so because he values the administrative abilities of these men, not because he wants to have them as advocates of the business world in the executive. (His attitude to the steel industry has made this abundantly clear.) Kennedy is applying a new principle in selecting members of the power elite for service in Washington: the men he chooses must not be defenders of the social status quo, but liberal pragmatists of the "new frontier." (There is hardly a speech in which Kennedy does not refer to the great "unfinished business" before the country.)

Perhaps the most influential members of the power elite are the legal consultants to the investment bankers, or the investment bankers themselves, who have the best knowledge of the key personnel in the economy and an over-all view of the industrial potential. They are key figures in the interlocking of the political, industrial and military hierarchies. Men like McCloy, Clay, Allen Dulles, Dillon, Dewey, Brownell, and Acheson, belong to this group, as did the late John Foster Dulles. The rule is interchangeability. Generals like Clay or MacArthur become company presidents. Company presidents like the late Charles Wilson, McElroy, or McNamara become Defense Secretaries. Bankers like Aldrich and Whitney become ambassadors. A banker and repeated Cabinet member like Lewis Strauss bears the rank of an admiral. Generals like Gruenther and Bedell Smith occupy high civilian posts.

The British concept of "the Establishment" covers a broader group, but at the top it refers to the same kind of people as those described as the "power elite." In his *The American Establishment* (1962), written somewhat—but not altogether —tongue-in-cheek, Richard Rovere names McCloy as the former, Dean Rusk (now Secretary of State, previously of the Rockefeller Foundation) as the present "real chairman of the Establishment." McCloy's *curriculum vitae* reads, indeed, like an inventory of the key positions of the power elite. Rovere enumerates them: "Chairman of the Board of the Chase Manhattan Bank; once a partner in Cadwalader, Wickersham & Taft, and also in Cravath, de Gersdorff, Swaine & Wood . . . as well as, of course, Milbank, Tweed, Hope, Hadley & McCloy; former United States High Commissioner in Germany; former President of the World Bank; liberal Republican; Chairman of the Ford Foundation and the Council of Foreign Relations; Episcopalian." He was also Special Adviser on Disarmament to President Kennedy.

The members of the power elite have much in common socially: a rather conservative style of life, the same universities or military academies, and the same clubs. Often they are allied thanks to the almost dynastic marriage policy practiced by some of the old and wealthy families. Hardly any of them owe their posts to election.

Considering the power of the unions in American life, one may well ask why their leaders have not joined the ranks of the power elite as, in fact, they have not. They remain on that middle level where interests are the issue, not decisions affecting the nation. The nonpolitical tradition of the American unions explains a good deal; however, their exclusion from the inner power circle need not, and probably will not, be final.

America is far from being frozen in fixed institutions. Even the power elite, born of the unaccustomed primacy of foreign policy, is not the last word. Its composition can alter. America's problem in this century is to act competently without becoming torpid in the sphere of decision, politically paralyzed by the precarious balance of terror. The power elite at the top is likely to be a permanent structure, to the extent that anything in history is permanent. But its composition, its thinking, its attitude to the world and particularly to the rivalry with the other super-power, these points have not been finally determined. New forms of osmosis are conceivable. Under President Kennedy, for the first time, intellectuals from the universities are able to penetrate the power elite as members of the White House staff. The partition between this elite and American society remains permeable.

3.

The Self-correcting Capitalism

FOR the first time in human history, an economic system is contending with the problems not of scarcity but of abundance. American society is the first ever to be faced with the need to live with abundance as the normal human condition —in other words, to accept the abnormal as the normal. Could anything be easier, more attractive? For the normal condition of mankind has always been extreme poverty, so much so that Karl Marx could prophesy the inevitable growth of poverty leading to an equally inevitable revolutionary upheaval. Marx's theory of increasing poverty of the workers certainly made history, even if it has proved false in the event. Its greatest refutation is the society, of continental dimensions, which has developed as the United States of America. That society today presents a surface picture of fantastic, breath-taking abundance of goods and services.

In the past decade, the United States economy has been in the nature of a cornucopia incessantly showering its benefits on the consumer, who is the official sovereign of the affluent society. But, in that same period, developments have taken place which bear little relation to the social myths which still feed the American consciousness.

Since 1960, the annual gross national product has exceeded five hundred billion dollars. That is a staggering figure. In the seventeen years since the end of the Second World War, the total of goods and services produced in America approaches the six thousand billion dollar mark, eighty per cent of which has gone into private consumption—personal enjoyment of life or its securing for the future. The way this enjoyment of life has been diffused is in itself a silent revolution. America has achieved the closest approximation to a classless society of any modern nation. It would be inaccurate to call it a middle-class society, because this concept is tied to the spatial analogy of the social pyramid. American society, as presently constituted, is more analogous to two pyramids (one inverted) joined at the base, their apices pointing down and up.

The lower apex represents the really poor, whose annual income is under $1,000. Like their counterpart at the upper apex—starting with an annual income of over $7,500—they constitute some ten per cent of the population. In between lies the great mass of eighty per cent, which significantly does *not* resemble a pyramid tapering off toward the top with the number decreasing as the size of the income increases. A better picture of this middle group would be that of an old-fashioned pitcher, bulging in the middle; there is the low-income group, with incomes between $1,000 and $3,000, making up twenty-seven per cent; next, those with incomes between $3,000 and $5,000, making up thirty-two per cent—a larger percentage than the first, whereas in every European society it is smaller; and finally those with incomes between $5,000 and $7,000, making up twenty-one per cent. If the optimistic editors of *Fortune* are right, the picture can develop back to a simple pyramid by 1970, except that it would be an inverted pyramid. They say, in their joint study, *Markets of the Sixties,* that, by then, forty-five per cent of all families will be earning over $7,500; thirty-eight per cent between $7,500 and $4,000, and the remainder under $4,000. That would really reverse every historical tradition since the disappearance of primitive communism. It would be the fulfillment of the affluent society, in which, again according to *Fortune,* over half of all personal income would be discretionary, that is, available for other uses than purchase of basic necessities.

But the near-classlessness of American society does not mean the absence of many wealthy people in America. Robert J. Lampman, in his *The Share of the Top Wealth-holders in National Wealth, 1922-1956* (published in 1961), reveals the astonishing fact that one per cent of the population owns twenty-eight per cent of the national wealth, and that this has not changed since 1933, when Roosevelt launched the New Deal. But this wealth has lost its social sting, because the superabundance of consumer goods has made differences in standards of living more and more painlessly relative.

To make a deity of insatiable consumption, with its hundred greedy arms reaching out to satisfy its desires, Americans have had to travel a long way from the Puritan beliefs of the Founding Fathers in their economic thinking. The Founding Fathers would have regarded their heirs' practices as little short of blasphemy. For the accepted American theory of today is to seek abundance for the individual because it is the source of the dynamism which keeps the tremendous mechanism of production running. The consumer, by consuming, fulfills a sacred duty. A special industry, with headquarters concentrated on Madison Avenue (and which, therefore, takes its name from that thoroughfare, as French diplomacy takes its name from the Quai d'Orsay), facilitates the performance of this duty by expending a boundless wealth of imagination on methods of constantly enlarging the horizon of human wants and their satisfaction.

The statistical datum that the American standard of living has risen by twenty-five per cent since 1941 insufficiently describes the consequence of this cult of consumption. For, in 1941, the American standard of living was already high, so that the further increase lies in the realm of abundance, taking human want as the norm. Never before has sophistication of demand so far down the social scale constituted the basis of production as it has in America within the last decade.

The magic by which hitherto unsuspected needs are aroused is consumer credit—supplemented by the fertile imagination of the advertising experts of Madison Avenue. Seventy per cent of the annual income of all consumers is owed in the form of installment payments and mortgages. Indebtedness is creative—the whole Puritan idea of the sanctity of thrift is turned upside down. The confidence of credit-giver and moneylender appears to be as unlimited as the consumer's needs are insatiable. Both parties believe in the eternal upward movement of the economy and concomitant job security; both have cast off the pessimism which might have remained in their unconscious as a legacy of the frightful depression of the thirties. And so, on time payments, people buy swimming pools and furs, air tickets to Europe in summer, winter vacations in sunny Florida, Hawaii or the Caribbean, ski vacations on the Canadian border or in Colorado—all after satisfying their needs in the way of cars, furniture, ever larger refrigerators, color television, and, finally, food and clothing. Thus, it is quite common for an American family to own its own home and car (or two cars), as well as the many electrical appliances which eliminate manual work in the running of a household—in order to subject itself the more readily to the ceaseless fascination of a pleasure industry promoted by advertising.

Already, three out of every five American families own homes. The horizontal trend which has replaced the vertical trend of the skyscrapers is covering the great green spaces around the cities with the individual houses of suburbia. Suburbia is a way of life. Moreover, land outside the cities is cheaper and therefore constitutes an important economic condition for making private home ownership available to the masses. In the family-centered society which America has become in recent years, and which now increases at the rate of three million yearly, suburbia is regarded as the ideal place to rear children. The price is the loss of the "city air which makes one free"; a minority of suburbanites already regret this and have moved back to the city where no one need know his neighbor if he does not want to. In suburbia, neighborliness acts as a potent instrument of conformity. In this world of carefully mowed lawns there already lives one-third of the nation—sixty million people.

What will the American society of the future look like? If it continues on its present path, its characteristics can already be predicted. But even if it did not take that path, the basic traits would remain, though their position in the scale of values might be different. The present scale of values, dominated by the greedy deity of consumption, would change. What would remain would be the tendency to depart ever farther from the simple tastes of America's early days. Since basic needs are satisfied as a matter of course, the full economy has to make use of artificially induced demands which tend to make luxury an everyday affair. The American consumer spends an average of fifty million dollars annually on champagne, eight million dollars on caviar, four hundred million dollars on swimming pools, 170 million dollars on outboard motors, twenty billion dollars on vacation and weekend trips inside America, and, if this may still be called consumption, places 2.5 billion dollars in bets on races.

It may be distressing that primacy, in this sophisticated consumption, is so obviously not given to the needs of the mind. But the intellectual may console himself with the reflection that for some time now more tickets have been bought for concerts of classical music than for football games. The priority enjoyed by private consumption over all other economic motives leads inevitably to rising demands in regard to quality and style. It does not lead to the grey monotony of the standardized article of Orwell's nightmare Utopia, but, on the contrary—to cite a curious illustration—to Sears, Roebuck sending buyers to the fashion shows of the Paris *haute couture* (a practice initiated in 1956). The American working woman in Christian Dior dresses? This vision of the future pushes consumer enthusiasm just a little too far. Nevertheless, the abundance of goods makes the mass consumer increasingly selective.

In the matter of food, for instance, the variety available is so enormous that the local supermarkets can compare with the most select food shops of Europe. High employment and taxation, between them, have destroyed the conditions in which service was a recognized social category. Only Negroes still perform this type of work, and they will continue to do so only so long as the chances of advancement afforded to the white population are denied them. Nevertheless, services of a kind are in fact to be bought in the supermarkets; they are built into the frozen vegetables and meat cuts, which are already cleaned, cut and partially cooked. To see the women leaving the supermarkets in their cars filled with tall, rounded paper bags, like crazy fragments of ancient temple pillars; to see this whole demonstration of abundance on the shelves and counters, one might think that food played a disproportionate part in the family budget. The contrary is true. Statistics show that the average American family spends only about one-half as much of its income on food as its European counterpart.

In clothing, the cultivation of taste and style is evident. Differences between custom tailoring and mass production in men's clothing are becoming ever less noticeable. But the somewhat disquieting prospect that everyone will soon be dressed like a lord is reduced by the American fondness for casual attire, especially in suburbia.

In their style of life, the democratized landed gentry of suburbia have adopted a number of upper-class practices of former days: there is greater sociability and more invitations to each other's homes, and these in turn influence consumption—women's fashions, for instance—in the direction of increasing fastidiousness. The building style of the low houses which cover hundreds of acres around metropolitan areas is space-squandering, as only a nation that is also a continent can afford. Suburbia would be unthinkable without the automobile, the instrument of mobility. The never-ending stream of cars on the roads is an image of the dynamism of an economy which has made production the goal of life.

To want to do away with poverty is almost like wanting to do away with death. Never yet has a society existed without the dark undertones of want. The fear of destitution is, as it were, built into capitalism as an indispensable creative driving force. A free society in which the individual need no longer fear destitution has never so far existed. There have been hierarchical, patriarchal, precapitalist societies which have forestalled this danger. Now, in the post-capitalist era of which America affords the first example, the danger of destitution has disappeared.

Poverty, as a physical state of individuals and groups, has not been eliminated—not yet. But it is confined to isolated pockets which, for one reason or another, have been excluded from the production momentum. They are constantly shrinking islands in an affluent society. Only a generation ago they were not islands but the broad base of the income pyramid; at that time seventy-five per cent of all American families earned under $2,000 a year. At the end of the Second World War, one-third of all American families still earned under $2,000 a year. Today, the proportion is one-sixth. Soon the hard core of private poverty will be made up only of alcoholics, the sick and the crippled. At the present time, old people who have been left alone also belong to the poor, living on the crumbs of welfare measures which America has adopted since the New Deal of the thirties (which is why they do not starve). Other underprivileged groups include farmers whose yield is below marginal utility and who are gradually being squeezed out by mechanized agriculture (the President's farm message of January 31, 1962, stated that of 3.5 million farmers, 1.5 million accounted for eighty-seven per cent of the total production); small businessmen who have gone bankrupt because the irresistible advance toward giant concerns has pitilessly ridden them down; people in depressed areas who remain there, though they can never expect anything there but poverty, out of inertia or for reasons of sentiment; and finally, the racially handicapped, the Negroes, Indians and Puerto Ricans, in transition toward participation in the opportunities for advancement which generally exist in this society where individual poverty has ceased to be a structural element of the economy.

But there is a quite different kind of poverty in America. Its existence is all the more disconcerting by reason of its glaring contrast with private prosperity. The cult of consumption is fed, even artificially aroused, by the profit motive. And the profit motive is regarded as its own justification because it begets production—which, in turn, according to accepted doctrine, is the safeguard of full employment and prosperity uncheckered by depression. But the cult of consumption has led to a social disequilibrium in which private and public wealth are glaringly, absurdly out of proportion.

While private wealth is augmented by affluence, since otherwise consumption would be slowed down by satiation, comparative poverty reigns in the public sector. Individual wealth in America has increased at an amazing rate since the end of World War II, thanks to the rapid advances in technology. The gross national product has risen to gigantic dimensions. But only a minute part of this wealth is channeled into public services. Of the mere twenty per cent of the gross national product diverted to public expenditures on the three levels of federal, state, and municipal government, a much larger proportion goes into defense and related expenses (such as foreign aid) than into the maintenance, expansion, and qualitative improvement of the public sector, without which the private affluent society would assuredly collapse. Education, basic research, roads, airports, hospitals, provision of power, public housing and slum clearance, and public transport in the huge cities, are some of the areas affected. Serious deficiencies have appeared in all these services, and they are viewed with rising concern.

Two well-known Harvard professors have made the contrast between private wealth and public poverty the starting point of a far-reaching critique of American civilization. The crux of the matter is of course the question of priorities, which, in turn, is dependent on a society's accepted scale of values. The contrast to which we have referred arises out of a Carthaginian value system, and its critics point out that Rome conquered Carthage long before the collapse of antiquity took place.

Arthur M. Schlesinger, now a special assistant at the White House, represents a school of political science which calls for a "qualitative" liberalism, as against the "quantitative" liberalism of the thirties needed to shield society against the human devastation of the depression. The latter objective has since been attained; what remains is to improve the *quality* of American civilization. Schlesinger wrote in 1956: "Our shops overflow with gadgets and gimmicks; consumer goods of ever-increasing ingenuity and luxuriance pour out of our ears. But our schools become more crowded and dilapidated, our teachers more weary and underpaid, our playgrounds more crowded, our cities dirtier, our roads more teeming and filthy, our national parks more unkempt, our law enforcement more overworked and inadequate. And we wonder why, for example, we have a growing problem of juvenile delinquency!"

This disequilibrium in the affluent society serves John Kenneth Galbraith as the point of departure for a searching, and often caustic examination of the conventional economic thinking to which America still, in the main, subscribes. His *Affluent Society,* which appeared in 1958, may well play as great a role as Keynes' teachings did a generation ago. Galbraith is the first economist to draw conclusions from the fact that abundance has become the characteristic feature of the American economy, not scarcity and want, as in the days when the pessimistic doctrines of the classic economists were developed. He maintains, therefore, that the American affluent society, as it has emerged since the Second World War, cannot continue to adhere to the economic thinking which prevailed when it first undertook its fantastic upward surge. The achievement of abundance carries within it the seed of its own destruction.

It is not always so clear, as in the case of the automobile, that public poverty eventually injures private consumption, and can even make private affluence meaningless. Without streets, highways, traffic regulations, parking facilities, police protection and—unfortunately—hospitals, the private ownership of powerful vehicles would be pointless and indeed dangerous. The more goods consumed, the more wrappings and containers there are to be thrown away, and the more essential is municipal garbage collection—a service which in the United States is run with curiously outmoded equipment. "If the appropriate sanitation services are not provided," writes Galbraith, "the counterpart of increasing opulence will be deepening filth." More subtle is the connection between private affluence and public poverty in such fields as education and basic research. Here the disproportion in expenditures between the public and the private sectors directly threatens the national rate of growth.

Under the surface of the affluent society there operate currents of self-destruction of which the neglect of the public services is only a symptom. Public services in the broadest sense always suffer most under inflationary pressure. The abandonment of public service posts with fixed salaries, or at any rate of those which require highly qualified personnel, is an unmistakable sign of the erosion resulting from the constant rise in the cost of living, the gnawing away at the purchasing power of the currency. Employment in private industry, where wages and salaries tend to keep pace with rising prices, is, today, a better insurance against devaluation than any function in the public service. It provides greater economic security. In the past the contrary was true.

The high plateau of American prosperity is bordered on the one side by the precipice of depression, on the other by inflation. Of the two dangers, inflation, as we now know, is the greater and more permanent danger, arising, as it does, most immediately out of the very nature of abundance. It is the shadow accompanying abundance and it is no longer merely the small shadow which a man casts as he walks in the street in the blinding light of noon.

Between 1955 and 1959, when prices rose constantly and the purchasing power of the dollar declined, the shadow became very long. It is hard to rid oneself altogether of the fear that this shadow, though at first only the consequence of the excessive brightness of the continuing boom—interrupted only by mild "recessions"—may in time blot out the brightness altogether.

Almost every year, the cost of living is higher than the last. The cost-of-living index rises or remains at a high level. High prices, but also high wages and salaries—all this seemed at first, at the beginning of the second half of the fifties, only the expression of a vertiginous expansion of production in an apparently inexhaustible diversity of forms—what could be termed a demand inflation, the reverse side of the boom, with its pressure on labor, goods and raw materials. It was therefore expected that inflation could be controlled by the classic monetary expedient of tightening credit. The Federal Reserve Bank raised the bank rate no fewer than half a dozen times,

but prices went on rising, even—against all economic logic—
when the last recession began. Prices have to fall in times of
recession, since the demand decreases. But American prices
did not fall. It was as though surgeons—in this case the orthodox credit cutters—were to open up a patient and find
hitherto unknown organs. They would aggravate his condition without discovering the cause of the malady. The policy
of dear money had unfortunate social consequences: it seriously affected small and weak firms but hardly touched the
big ones. It thus involuntarily encouraged the trend toward
ever greater agglomerations of economic power. The mammoth firms grew even bigger, the weaker firms went bankrupt. The spiral of wages, profits and prices was not brought
under control, while on the other hand, such things as school
construction, already tragically overdue in this wealthy country, were still further retarded.

The unsuccessful operation of 1957 led to the realization
that the American economy had developed structures which
bore little relation to the traditional theories of the free market. Congressional hearings and expert investigations revealed
these new structures. The economy was seen to have a completely new anatomy. Monetary means had failed to halt inflation because the price formation which it was designed to
affect was taking place quite differently from anything that
classic economic theory had ever anticipated. Inflation, it was
now realized, was not simply the result of excessive prosperity. The productive forces responsible for this prosperity
were also responsible for breeding inflation, not because they
were forced to by the operations of the free competitive market, but, on the contrary, because they had taken the process
of price formation into their own hands. The process has
been expressed by the concept of "administered prices," a term
coined by the economist, Gardiner C. Means.

Administered prices are prices which are not determined by
the free market but by the producers, by administrative

means, that is, from above (assuming the individual consumer to be below). The consumer ceases to be the reputed sovereign in the game of supply and demand; he ceases to pull the strings of the economy. The producers determine their own prices.

On the price-determining side are the mammoth firms and the "sellers" of labor, the unions. While market prices remain firm or fall, administered prices may rise, even during a generalized economic recession, thereby producing an "administered inflation." As a result, increased productivity no longer automatically benefits the consumer by lowering prices. That is the potential seed of self-destruction in the affluent society. And if inflation comes to be taken as inevitable, then —to cite Professor Henry C. Wallich of Yale University—a number of unfortunate consequences will ensue. "Saving habits of consumers and businessmen's decisions governing output and investment are distorted. Speculative motivations displace those of the market and production. Growth of production suffers, and the expansion, at first stimulated by production, slows down. Meanwhile the international position of the dollar is undermined."

The American economic system does not, it is true, correspond to the now somewhat naive notion of free competition between independent entrepreneurs for the benefit of the sovereign consumer, but neither is it a controlled economy. This is perhaps the greatest challenge confronting a free society: to curb abundance where it begins to disintegrate in unregulated competition between productivity and group claims, but voluntarily and without odious controls.

Leading economists realize that the American economy is moving away from the type conceived by Adam Smith no less than from the type conceived by Karl Marx. Neither the concept of the free market nor that of class war covers the structure which has developed in the boom years since the Second World War. Economists have coined the new word "oligopoly" for it, in whose ugly sound there perhaps echoes the horror which grips many an observer confronted with the new picture of the economy. The market, it appears, is governed by a few large economic units—some five hundred huge concerns and the giant labor unions, for the most part allied (with the exception of one of the largest groups, the transport workers). A new power structure is thus emerging. The economic giants use their power to establish prices, wages and production levels independently of the play of demand and supply. A silent solidarity, which has also been called a secret love affair between capital and labor, has become basic to the system. Big industry and labor unions together form the oligopoly. A strike takes place for higher wages, and after a while the higher rates are approved—ostensibly unwillingly —and not long after comes the price rise, allegedly on grounds of the wage rise but in fact far outstripping it. The managerial hierarchies on both sides of the labor process have found a profitable *modus vivendi*. Their interests interlock.

The ramifications of this community of interests go beyond the wage-price problem; they obstruct the establishment of competitive enterprises; they affect measures taken to absorb the shocks of automation; and they may work for higher protective tariffs. The big business managers are interested in high prices because they have options on stock in their own concerns and high prices mean high profits which also drive up the market price of shares. Prices are set in such a way that they produce profits even when the concern is working at diminishing capacity (instead of prices being lowered to stimulate demand, acocrding to conventional theory). The steel industry, for instance, by this means, doubled its prices in the space of ten years. Organized labor had to be mollified in the face of the high profits. That was done by means of annual wage increases, combined with increased benefits, which again drove up the spiral.

The love affair of the oligopoly was carried on within the

great production agglomerations, in the steel industry, in coal, oil, chemicals, the automobile industry and heavy industry generally. Around these agglomerations there is still genuine competition among smaller firms which do not have a fully organized labor force to deal with. But the real power structure is composed of those concentrations of capital and labor before which the consuming public is forced to abdicate. The public does not feel injured by such abdication, because the cornucopia of consumer goods could only have become so apparently inexhaustible as a result of mass production on this enormous scale. And it may not be too high a price for society to pay for burying the hatchet of class conflict.

The "affair" between the two industrial forces was bitterly tested in the hundred-day steel strike of 1959. Circumstances which had long been building up, combined with various accidental factors, made this longest and most costly strike in industrial history a turning point in the development of American society. New balances of power began to emerge. The solidarity of interests was ruptured, because its basis, the administered wage-price-profit spiral, had ceased to function; it could not be turned any further. The public, led by Congress, which directed its investigatory powers against the industrial power blocs, came to see the responsibility of administered prices for the rising cost of living. (European observers liken administered prices to cartel agreements, but the comparison is not quite exact. They represent a monopoly by reason of the size of the concerns involved; the big producers assimilate their prices by tacit agreement, a practice against which the antitrust laws are powerless, and the smaller ones follow suit.) The Eisenhower administration, desiring to protect the dollar, launched an information campaign on the subject of the strike which made it hard for the steel industry, in view of its own high profits, to compensate for new wage increases by still higher profits, as it had previously done.

At the same time, the political climate was developing unfavorably for the unions. The swing of the pendulum from power to counter-power, which in America never stands still, was against them, just as in the second quarter of the century it had been for them and against the power inroads of industry and high finance. The period, which closed under Roosevelt in the thirties, saw the rise to power of the unions. The National Labor Relations Act of 1935 was their Magna Carta, recognizing them as the legal representatives of labor in collective bargaining, and at the same time removing them from the purview of the antitrust laws. This was American industry's only legal monopoly. It soon became apparent that the unions, as a mighty monopolistic force, were able to cripple vital sectors of the national economy. Moreover, since they subsidized candidates for elective office or procured them votes —mostly, but not exclusively, candidates of the Democratic party—they were able to win indirect political power, such as the other side already possessed.

In 1947, a kind of conservative counter-revolution set in. The unions had their wings clipped. The Taft-Hartley Act gave the President the legal right to interrupt any strike that threatened to bring about a national emergency. Individual states introduced legislation providing for the "right to work," which prohibited the compulsory organization of workers by unions—though in most states overtly anti-union measures are not popular. After a sensational two-year congressional investigation had revealed corrupt and terroristic conditions in some of the unions—underworld practices curiously inappropriate in a labor movement—Congress in 1959 approved a reform bill which represented a serious political setback for the unions. The Labor-Management Reporting and Disclosure Act, carried by a Congress dominated by Democrats, drastically curbed the powers of the unions. The legislators had been subjected to strong grassroots pressure and many workers, however discreetly, had intimated their desire for a curtailment of the powers of union officials.

The new act was directed against coercive picketing tactics, against the boycott of nonparticipants, against physical violence whereby plants were "organized" for the unions, against the financial corruption in the administration of union funds uncovered by the McClellan Committee. It checked the spread of union organization throughout the economy, but it did not affect the core of union power, their monopoly of the labor supply within the big industrial concentrations.

The representatives of management felt they could take advantage of the situation. They not only refused to raise wage rates, but they also challenged the unions to a great trial of strength: was this not the moment to set back the clock of social history? The crux of the labor conflict was not the monetary level of wages, but the changing of the work rules which industry had made a precondition for every wage increase. These were the prerogatives of factory workers, established by contract in 1947 and never since called in question. Management, like the factory owner before it, wanted to be sole master on the factory grounds. And because such a claim challenged labor positions gained a quarter-century earlier, it provoked direct resistance on the part of the unions. In consequence, the nation as a whole was faced with the appalling spectacle of two giants recklessly fighting out their duel as though there existed no public interest. The new structure of mammoth organizations became more evident than ever before in this state of war where each was too strong to concede defeat. The economic power blocs had become stronger than the nation could afford.

This recognition constitutes another turning point. The clock of social history will not be turned back, but forward. Now the power pendulum will swing in favor of neither the one nor the other power group—neither labor nor industry— but in favor of the "third force," preventive intervention on behalf of the public interest. Even a Republican like Nelson Rockefeller, one of the leaders of a party which opposes government interference, supported the proposal that the President should be empowered to impose compulsory arbitration in labor disputes. There will be a closer tie between Big Business, Big Labor and Big Government. This association dissolves the concealed affair between industry and labor. A triangular relationship has proved necessary.

This was confirmed early in 1962, when Secretary of Labor Goldberg stated in Chicago that henceforth, when the Government moved into collective bargaining, it would assert the national interest and not simply mediate. He added cogently that the issues in labor-management affairs had become "far too complex, far too potent and far too influential on the rest of the society to be resolved on the old resting ground of clash of selfish interests."

But the structure that has become apparent through all these developments is here to stay: the mammoth firms, the huge industrial and commercial concerns. Not just a type of economy, but also a way of life, perhaps even a philosophy, make up the collective institutions of the immensely productive American economy in this second half of the twentieth century. Let us look at them a little more closely.

The mammoth firm is the result of the collectivization of social and economic life, and this collectivization, apparently irresistible, is the result of the trend towards larger units. Larger units mean greater and more efficient production. They also mean the hegemony of the organization.

In one of the most significant books of recent times, *The Organization Man* (published in 1956), William H. Whyte describes life inside the great economic organizations, as Maeterlinck once described the life of insects. "Organization" is used to designate a company or corporation large enough to claim the rank of an all-embracing institution. Of course "the organization" is also a generic term for all kinds of huge social mechanisms in which the individual can be absorbed.

Whyte includes among "organization men" officers in the armed services, air-line pilots, ministers in the ecclesiastical hierarchies, doctors in big hospitals, scientists in research laboratories (particularly those of the Atomic Energy Commission), lawyers in the Wall Street legal factories and, of course, all government officials. But what is new is that industry, too, is increasingly taking on the features of an administration which peremptorily, if beneficently, lays hands on the individual.

An individual does not belong to the category of "organization men" because he is a salary-earner in a big firm. He is an organization man because he has given himself to the organization as to an order, because he owes it fealty, because he is more incorporated in it than he is in a social class, the circle of his friends, or the native scene from which he emerged. The managerial corps of the economic organizations are rootless in their own land, like diplomats who are transferred by their governments from one foreign post to another. Company executives—directors and their successors—are transferred every few years to the organization's various production or administrative centers scattered all over the country. Their only roots are in the interchangeability of suburbia, their specific form of life. Here, in housing projects far from the cities, they are everywhere equally at home, they find similar groups of organization men when they move in, and then leave again, each as the distant head office of the organization disposes.

How do the company elite live in suburbia? Whyte puts it: "To hoard possessions is frowned upon; books, silverware and tea services are constantly rotated, and the children feel free to use one another's bikes and toys without asking. 'We laughed at first at how the Marxist society had finally arrived,' one executive says, 'but I think the real analogy is to the pioneers.'" Marxism, pioneers—or a new Middle Ages? William Whyte sees in the strong sense of emotional security provided by group membership a clear analogy between the ideological role of the big organizations and the structure of medieval society. He explains, with a touch of sarcasm: "Not that we should go back to all this, mind you. The job, to paraphrase, is to recreate the belongingness of the Middle Ages. What with the Enlightenment, the Industrial Revolution and other calamities, the job is immensely more difficult than it was in those simpler days. But with new scientific techniques we can solve the problem." An artificially created Middle Ages? "We must learn consciously to achieve what once came naturally. We must form an elite of skilled leaders who will guide men back, benevolently, to group belongingness."

The author hopes that this will be possible without loss of the inner freedom of the organization man. He even gives him frank advice on how to withstand the total demands of the organization (Orwell's Big Brother). But this is the human type which will inevitably determine American direction in the next decades. And America's social form is the precursor of the Western world. It is a few laps ahead of the rest. Max Weber traced Anglo-Saxon capitalism back to Calvin's doctrine of predestination, to the impulse emerging out of the Calvinistic hallowing of personal economic success. This individualism based on the Protestant ethos is a thing of the past. It has been replaced by the voluntary collectivism of the great corporations, by the "social ethos" in which the organization's claims on an individual's fealty is rationalized. The remarkable phenomenon of a collectivist capitalism is emerging, a further development of what James Burnham a decade ago revealed as the "managerial revolution."

Gardiner C. Means has evolved a theory of "collective enterprise," as he boldly calls the big concern which has replaced the private enterprise—that embodiment of capitalism, of "free enterprise"—as the dominant structural form. He draws the conclusion, which at one time would have been pilloried as "unAmerican," that the profit motive should be removed from the considerations of management. He argues that the logic of collective enterprise assigns to the men at the top the role of arbiters between opposing interests: between stockholders, labor and the public. The principle on which they perform this duty should be the optimum use of resources. High profits as the financial bait for corporate management contravenes this principle. On the other hand, it would be unrealistic not to take management's profit motive into consideration. The solution, for Means, is to change the bonus system. The current practice is to reward the leaders of industry by options on shares, which make high profits attractive. This does not serve the public interest. The lure of high profits must therefore be abolished by making incomes at the top independent of profit. Means proposes that top management should receive special indemnities for enhanced achievement in the optimum use of resources.

The constituent principle of an economy dominated by industrial organizations is the breaking up of property. Its most important consequence is the separation of control from property. To wield economic power it is no longer necessary to own the means of production. Those who own them have for the most part no control over their operation, or only nominal control. American capitalism has ceased to be based on property.

This transference of economic power to new holders has been accomplished in stages, the last of which has only just begun. Two of the stages were completed in the first three decades of the present century. Up to 1914, the American economy was dominated by the ultra-plutocracy which had characterized it since 1870 and which still, perhaps, colors its image abroad. In that earlier period, the distinction between factory owner and management had already been made, but the owner, as the majority stockholder, still exercised full authority over the personnel of management, and for the rest lived the life of a multimillionaire in the places of Newport or the North Shore of Long Island.

With the exception of a few families like the Fords, Du Ponts or Mellons, control through majority holdings generally lasted little more than a generation. Up to the opening of the thirties, the typical arrangement was divided control by stockholders and industrial managers. The stockholder could have a "working control" over the re-election of directors, based on his influence, even without possessing an absolute majority of stocks, but he was obliged to cooperate with management. This shackle, too, has been cast off in the last twenty-five years, control passing without restriction to management. Management makes up its own slates of directors; these are self-perpetuating; they select their own successors. Ownership is split up among millions of shareholders whose power is only nominal. The real power is in the hands of the managerial hierarchy. Management alone has the power of decision, the power to take the economic initiative. The shareholders are merely the passive recipients of the wealth which the giant organization scatters.

Adolf A. Berle, one of the foremost experts on the theory and practice of the economic structure, points out, in his *Power without Property* (1959), that a fourth stage of distribution of power is being ushered in, which threatens the dominant role of management. The ownership of shares is continually expanding, becoming more "democratic," as it were—there are now some 12.5 million shareholders in the country. But the acquisition of shares by fiduciary organizations representing shareholders, a still relatively new practice, again suddenly concentrates the right of personal participation which goes with the ownership of shares. New mechanisms—pension trustees, fiduciary institutions, insurance managements—now aggregate voting rights. They—the fiduciary organizations—are thus in a position to influence the selection of the top personnel of the giant corporations. How this power will be used in the future, and whether it will be used, cannot yet be predicted. What is certain is that the rift between property and power is now accomplished. The owner of a pension claim, an insurance policy, or mutual funds, has a right to a specific sum of money which has lost every real connection with productive economic processes. He no longer knows where his money comes from. Berle comments: ". . . divorce between men and industrial 'things' is becoming complete. A Communist revolution could not accomplish that more completely. Certainly it could not do so with the same finesse."

The facts themselves impose an analogy with the structure of the Soviet collective economy. Could it be that the rivalry, the economic strife between the United States and the Soviet Union is really nothing but a family quarrel between two collective systems? Berle says on this score: "The difference lies in the fact . . . that the [Soviet] political State exercises the power factor now gradually but steadily being aggregated under the American system in nonpolitical but equally impersonal fiduciary institutions." Before we look into this comparison, let us ask what kind of man is the propertyless capitalist, the "organization man"? Whyte speaks of the new Middle Ages in the sense of firm integration in a group. Another social scientist advises ambitious managers to read Machiavelli's *Prince,* or Gratian's *Handbook for Courtiers.* All this indicates that the profit motive has already taken second place. Not that it has been altogether superseded by nobler instincts. But what takes first place is no longer the acquisition of wealth, which in any case is limited by taxation and consequently made less attractive, but power, prestige and position. The distinction between economic and political bureaucracies tends to become blurred. With the enormous incomes of company presidents (amounting to over $100,000 a year), there is a shift to the prestige value of income. The salary level is still the touchstone of success; but salary is now regarded as the tangible symbol of success instead of, as in the past, success being valued because it brings with it a higher salary. For above the $100,000 mark, taxes slice off so much as to make higher salaries practically pointless. The highest salaries are, in a sense, purely symbolic.

The modern industrial manager is a far more complex individual than the independent, daring entrepreneur of the classic age of capitalism. He has to know the imponderables which help or hinder a man's advance in the great organizational pyramid. He has to be able to play the diplomat, the psychologist, the courtier. He has to sublimate his instinct for possession. The public consensus as to what society expects of those who wield economic power restricts his actions hardly less than those of government officials. What this "public consensus" means is illustrated by Berle. As we know, public services such as railroads, telephone, telegraph, gas, and electricity, are operated in the United States by private industry. But if the American Telephone and Telegraph Company, for instance, should take advantage of its technical power to tap telephone conversations or to collect private information from its cable service, it would lose so much in the public estimation that government action would inevitably follow which might end this private domain for good. If the "conscience" of the firm breaks down, the State steps in. In this pragmatic, unplanned fashion the Federal Government has developed a number of supervisory and planning agencies since the end of the last century, and these have been loosely, but durably superimposed on a previously unregulated economy. This network of government agencies, like the powers developed by the State itself, is the unplanned result of circumstance. Americans, for whom every concentration of power is suspect, will give up a considerable dose of built-in anarchy in their society only under the exigencies of war.

The instruments of government intervention have developed slowly. Economically speaking, the individual may have been reduced to the status of a mutual fund stockholder, but politically he is in a position, through his legislators, to create these instruments. Once established, they function not as central control agencies, but in a diffused manner, rather like a referee on a playing field who intervenes if a player violates the rules of the game.

In this way, seven regulatory agencies supervise prices and business practices in the transport field (railroads, trucking, airlines and so on), gas and electricity supply, and the mass media of radio and television. The Federal Reserve Board controls currency, credit and interest rates, together with the Treasury, which administers the greatly augmented national debt. Government credits are extended to specific branches of the economy such as housing construction, merchant shipping, and the armaments industry. Farmers are subsidized. The Government piles up unimaginable quantities of farm surpluses. The oil companies receive depletion allowances to ensure a sufficient supply (as a result of which million-dollar fortunes are constantly being built up). Finally, the Government is also a producer in its own right, as when it builds hydroelectric dams, provides electricity for rural areas, establishes the research centers of the Atomic Energy Commission, and, of course, embarks on the special projects of the Defense Department. Congress fixes minimum wage rates.

Were this control network to be tightened instead of deliberately left in the hands of scattered agencies—and it will surely become more concentrated in the future—then the power of the giant corporations would be faced with the equally powerful planning authority of the Federal Government. Economic power is already divided between the production hierarchy and the government hierarchy, even though the former very properly possesses the greater part. The giant corporation is far too comprehensive not to have to plan in its turn, and it does have to plan with an eye on the economy as a whole. That is why the term "private socialism" has been used—

socialist procedures for capitalist ends. The analogy with Soviet State capitalism directed by economic commissariats is striking indeed.

Obscured by ideological differences, remarkable structural similarities have developed between the United States and the Soviet Union. Both systems have great administrative pyramids which direct production. In both systems, the economic initiative lies with the manager type, concerned about his career, his prestige and his pension, and no longer with the individual entrepreneur type. Capital formation in both systems is determined by the administrative pyramid (three-fifths of industrial capital formation in the United States is based on retained earnings). Production units in the Soviet Union operate in accordance with plans issued by the totalitarian State, while in the United States they operate within the pluralist framework of a few hundred big concerns. The American system thus possesses far greater flexibility in meeting private consumer needs, whereas it is inordinately slow in detaching portions of the gross national product for the benefit of public and social services, as we have seen. The precise contrary is true of the Soviet Union. But both sides have this in common, that they recognize these contrary weaknesses and seek to rectify them. The differences between the American and Soviet economic systems—particularly in the post-Stalin era—begin outside organization. Organization, in the two cases, serves different political philosophies. Were the only issue that of economic organization, there need be no irreconcilable antagonism between the two countries.

Since Khrushchev's visit to the United States in the fall of 1959, an open, unconcealed rivalry between the economic systems of the United States and the Soviet Union has become the dominant fact of world politics. The economic race has taken its place alongside the arms race. Khrushchev has made the Communist and the democratic capitalist systems rationally comparable. That is his contribution to the history of ideologies. The standard of comparison is productivity, the rate of growth of both social and economic orders. Khrushchev proclaims the transition from socialism to communism to be the building of an affluent society, a stage which America has already reached and which, Khrushchev feels, Russia will reach soon, going on to outdistance the American variety.

America takes the state of rivalry very seriously. How seriously may be judged by the more than thirty studies, undertaken by eminent specialists at the request of Congress, to form the basis for an extensive congressional investigation. From these studies there emerged a fact that a short time before would barely have gained credence: that Khrushchev's predictions were far from mere wishful thinking. But most of the economic experts cautioned against a forced race between the two world powers in respect of their respective rates of growth.

The gross national product of the Soviet Union at the end of the fifties was about two-fifths that of the United States, its production per capita of the population one-third. The Soviet rate of growth between 1950 and 1960 was six to seven per cent; the American rate only three per cent. The absolute annual increase in the Soviet gross national product is less than the American, but it could catch up and even surpass the American figure if the growth rates remained unchanged. If the Soviet rate remains four per cent higher than the American rates, then Khrushchev's aim would be achieved in twenty-four years; if three per cent higher, in thirty-one years; if two per cent higher, in forty-seven years; and if one per cent higher, in ninety-three years.

It is questionable whether the Soviet Union can maintain its present rate of growth, since this is largely the expression of an economic development originating well before the country had achieved a substantial degree of industrialization. American expert opinion is unanimous in opposing the adoption of the Soviet idea of a race in growth rates. A forced enhancement of the American rate to the present Soviet level would eliminate the principal difference between the two economic rivals: freedom of choice for the consumer. The inner strength of the American system, we are told—and it can hardly be denied—is that it is humanly more attractive. To sacrifice its human traits would indeed be a high price to pay for the satisfaction of raising the gross national product higher and higher.

Quite apart from this world rivalry, though prompted by it, doubts were being voiced by the end of the fifties as to whether the affluent society, which is also a spendthrift society, was on the right path. The growth rate had in fact declined; the Kennedy administration hopes the economy will achieve a stable growth rate of over 3.5 per cent. The seeds of self-destruction which thrive in abundance—depression and inflation—have become evident. The absurd contrast between private affluence and public poverty, in particular, has reinforced the suspicion that the American society has not reached the degree of perfection ascribed to it.

In his *Affluent Society,* John Kenneth Galbraith puts these questions in the most radical form and answers them just as radically. His aim is to drive the fetish of the managerial world, the deity of consumption, out of the temples of economic thought. He destroys the taboos of accepted economic theory by showing that it fails to take the affluent society into account, and that it is still imprisoned in the 150-year-old tradition of Ricardo, based on the premise that goods are scarce and poverty is man's fate. Only if this basic premise is correct is it meaningful to gear the economy simply to the production of more and more consumer goods. Only if this premise is correct is production the central aim.

Although America has achieved abundance for all—or nearly all—not by a revolutionary redistribution of income, but by an increase in productivity over the last decades (resulting from improved technology and organization), people act in the economic field as though only the constant increase of consumer goods can save society from poverty. According to this thinking, there must be no saturation point in consumption, and so advertising to the tune of some eleven billion dollars a year creates artificial needs, a synthetic demand. Galbraith writes: ". . . economic theory has managed to transfer the sense of urgency in meeting consumer need that once was felt in a world where more production meant more food for the hungry, more clothing for the cold, and more houses for the homeless, to a world where increased output satisfies the craving for more elegant automobiles, more exotic food, more erotic clothing, more elaborate entertainment—indeed, for the entire modern range of sensuous, edifying and lethal desires."

From the anachronism that production is necessary for production's sake, with the result that a synthetically created need is placed on the same level as an elementary one, there follow, for Galbraith, the weaknesses of an affluent society which has not yet fully understood itself: the artificial creation of needs, the imbalance between private consumption and the impoverishment of the public sector, which, in turn, leads to inflation and the decline of the growth rate (owing to a decline in the skilled labor force).

But in the malady lies the cure, at least as the economist sees it. If a balance could be achieved between production for profit and production for the needs of the community by means of a new type of taxation, the other defects in the system could also be remedied—creeping inflation and cyclical recessions with their inroads on economic security. Galbraith makes a number of thoroughly heretical proposals. He would sever the link between production and income (a vital artery of capitalism) by having unemployed workers paid almost the whole of their normal salaries in times of higher unemployment: a kind of "subsidy to idleness." He would shake off compulsion about full employment, a compulsion based on the worker's desire for security, but which in an affluent society can be satisfied only by artificially creating ever less important individual needs. So long as the production mechanism has to run at full capacity, not because its output is useful but because people know of no other way of sparing men the privations of unemployment, the danger of rising prices and constant inflation will persist. If a substitute can be found for production as a source of income, then the compulsion will be broken.

Galbraith thus proposes that the unemployed be paid the best part of their salaries, but only if unemployment has reached a high level. Otherwise, the measure would have an altogether inflationary effect. When unemployment declines, and more opportunities for employment are available, the amount of the subsidy would be reduced in order to counteract the increased cost of labor and the attraction of idleness. If, however, few were employed and many unemployed, the high compensation would stabilize purchasing power and reduce the fear of depression. Galbraith calls this a "cyclically graduated compensation."

This economic thinking can be translated into social practice only if subsidized idleness becomes respectable, only if it is recognized as a necessary consequence and a legitimate corollary of affluence—however shocking that would have appeared to the early Calvinists for whom the inner certainty of predestination could be achieved only by unceasing endeavor towards success. Economists like Galbraith believe that maximum production has ceased to be a vital goal of the economy. The key to the qualitative enhancement of society lies, in their view, in the transition from material investment to "investment in men," to investment in "resources of ability, intelligence and education."

This is a new dimension of the affluent society, reaching out beyond the problem of producing a sufficiency of goods (that problem being already resolved). Economically too, as these reflections show, America is the ever unfinished, ever self-correcting society.

4.

The Reconciliation of the Intellectuals

INTELLECTUALS are no longer necessarily left-wing, as they so definitely were in the thirties. This observation applies to America no less than to Europe. For example, during the second Eisenhower campaign against Adlai Stevenson (who dared to bring some of the finest qualities of an intellectual mind into the political arena), the Republican Party set up a committee to attract the "eggheads." In the hundred years of its history, the party had shown little enough interest in that species of man—and now it proceeded to create a body for the express purpose of winning his allegiance.

Where, then, are intellectuals at home, if not on the left? The American intellectual combated his own society for so long that he furnished anti-Americanism throughout the world with its choicest arguments. How does he react to that society today? Has something happened to him that he should deserve the attentions of the political party strategists? Has he changed?

The answer goes far beyond the ballot paper. The position of the American intellectual has changed indeed, just as the society has changed. Instead of rebellion and fruitful protest, there is assent. Instead of social estrangement and hostility, there is danger of social conformity, of intellectual orthodoxy. Independent thinkers, writers, even poets have become the exception. The rule is the socially integrated, sheltered intellectual, either openly or tacitly indebted to the status quo.

This development took place in the fifties, and it is perceptible even in the style of American writing. A closer look at the situation reveals some astonishing facts. America, it appears, is at a sophisticated stage of civilization; America is becoming conservative; ideological fires have spent themselves. At the same time we find an America in which education and taste have spread on a previously unimaginable scale, however much the discontented, the voluntary expatriates, or the confirmed heretics may still revolt against it.

Merle Curti has called the conflict between thought and action the "American paradox," a term he uses as the title of a book. He examines the very evident paradox of a society which in its origins was fed by the unity of thought and action, and yet has become so anti-intellectual. The explanation, acocrding to Professor Curti, lies in the leveling action of the pioneers, the acquisitiveness of an industrial society, and the rigidity of the society's sects. However, the tension with which the American intellectual reacted to his country's highly developed capitalist civilization was creative for three whole decades.

Out of this tension, there arose the great, rebellious works of the twenties and thirties, including the poems of Ezra Pound and T. S. Eliot (who at that period still counted as an American), the novels of Faulkner, Dos Passos, Scott Fitzgerald, Henry Miller, Sinclair Lewis, Thomas Wolfe, Hemingway, all of which developed the theme of the writer's estrangement from the society in which he lived. Whether living or not, these writers have found no equals among their younger successors (with the exception, perhaps, of Tennessee Williams, the playwright, who not so much protests against society, but evades it, investigating the darkest corners of the human condition at society's periphery). The "American paradox" is on the way to solution, and if this means less pain, it also means less literary greatness. Society has opened its arms to the intellectuals, and only a few have sought to evade the embrace.

Arthur Miller, whose play, *The Crucible,* about the witch trials at Salem in the seventeenth century was in fact an attack on McCarthyism, had difficulty, some years ago, in getting a passport for travel abroad. In this connection he was called before the Committee on UnAmerican Activities, where he refused to divulge the names of former Communists ameong his acquaintances. The next day, Marilyn Monroe, at that time still very much alive and the embodiment of the erotic fantasies of millions of Americans, announced her engagement to Arthur Miller. A wit commented that this was the greatest service anyone could have performed for American intellectuals.

But Arthur Miller's case is no longer typical. Mutual name-calling—"anti-intellectualism" on the one side and "anti-Americanism" on the other—no longer holds the center of the stage. The affluent society is no longer anti-intellectual, and the intellectual is no longer anti-American.

Of course, this relationship did not immediately develop from its opposite. George Kennan, that intellectual among diplomats, could still write recently: "I can think of few countries in the world where the artist, the writer, the composer or the thinker is held in such general low esteem as he is here in our country." Edmund Wilson sought to depict the position of the intellectual in society in *The Wound and the Bow*. The hero, Philoctetes, is a Greek warrior compelled to live out his life in solitude because of the stench given off by his wound. Nevertheless, his friends go back to him because they need his unerring magic bow. In somewhat the same way, American society needs the intellectual *qua* expert, but does not grant him anything even approaching the status of, say, a university professor in the German social hierarchy.

With the "lost generation" (a term coined by Gertrude Stein to describe the youthful Hemingway), a group of literary expatriates of the twenties living in physical separation from America, with the "sad young men" (like Fitzgerald, Hemingway, Dos Passos, Sherwood Anderson, and E. E. Cummings), there came about a radical break with American society. The first world war had hurled this generation "into the dark jaws of violence." Rootless as they were, their war experiences were bound up with Europe; their estrangement from their own society was complete. It led in the thirties to despair about the social order, to the uncompromising doctrine of the "two nations" of America propounded by John Dos Passos in *USA*. Raging over the execution of Sacco and Vanzetti, he wrote, spurning punctuation: "They have clubbed us off the streets they are stronger they are rich they hire and fire the politicians the newspaper editors the old judges the small men with reputations the college presidents the wardheelers . . . they hire the men with guns the uniforms the policecars the patrolwagons . . . they have built the electric chair and hired the executioner to throw the switch . . . all right we are two nations."

This class war between the two social nations within America no longer exists; the welfare State has made this kind of social protest pointless. To put it another way, it has subtilized the desires of the malcontents. Hence, those desires are harder to formulate. In any case, as Riesman has put it, "the reasons developed by intellectuals for the benefit of previous proletariats are of course quite irrelevant." From a literary standpoint, the Utopian content of socialist-communism is void.

In the latter part of the forties, directly after the end of the war, a new literary group, with independent, nonconformist views, seemed to enjoy an influence and an esteem such as their elders, of the post-war generation of 1920, had enjoyed before them. But for some reason not easy to elucidate, these extremely gifted post-war novelists—Norman Mailer, James Jones, John Horne Burns, Irwin Shaw, Paul Bowles, Truman Capote, Carson McCullers—some of them rebellious, brutally realistic, culling their material from war, sex, neurosis and sometimes even the slums, have receded both in standing and in achievement since the opening of the fifties. Norman Mailer, for instance, author of the violent war novel, *The Naked and the Dead,* is said by one reviewer, to have "dedicated himself to comfort, alcohol and marihuana." It is as though something essential to these writers has been lost in the present intellectual climate of America. There would seem to be a significant connection between their inadequacy and what *Time* has celebrated as the "reconciliation" of the intellectuals with America.

Though *Time* is ever prepared to approve the status quo, the facts it adduces are not in dispute. The rift between intellectuals and society has narrowed in consequence of a mutual rapprochement. *Time*'s star witness for the position of American intellectuals is Professor Jacques Barzun, who teaches history at Columbia. Actually, Barzun is highly critical of that position; what matters to Mr. Luce's editors, however, are the statements they can quote by Barzun and other intellectuals as evidence of a reconciliation.

The intellectuals of America, Barzun says, have today "won recognition in tangible ways beyond any previous group of their peers." Grumbling is out of date. Intellectuals who still grumble, Barzun says, "forget that the true creator's role, even in its bitterest attack, is to make us understand or endure life better. Our intellectuals do neither when they entice us to more self-contempt." The reference is to something that is already past, for by the end of the second world war, Barzun says, "it was no disgrace, no provincialism, to accept America and admire it . . . America was quite simply *the* world power, which means: the center of world awareness: it was Europe that was provincial."

Similarly one of the leading literary critics, Lionel Trilling, points out: "An avowed aloofness from national feeling is no longer the first ceremonial step into the life of thought . . .

For the first time in the history of the modern American intellectual, America is not to be conceived of as *a priori* the vulgarest and stupidest nation of the world."

The changed attitude of the intelligentsia to the social environment is also reflected in the rupture of its thirty-year-old alliance with organized labor. Intellectuals today are more likely to be found in the camp of the critics of the bureaucratic power of the unions, whereas, in New Deal days, intellectual blue-prints for a better society were bound up with an idealized notion of the working proletariat. Typical in this respect is the otherwise atypical Dos Passos, whose most recent novel, *Midcentury,* is a revolt against big labor. In the thirties, Dos Passos was a revolutionary anarchist. Now his philosophy has been described as a "libertarian Republicanism" akin to that of the late Senator Taft.

A new confidence is reflected in visions of the future, like this one of Mortimer Adler's: "In the long run, the new industrialization will produce an aristocratic society for the millions. We can produce Rome for the millions, or Athens for the millions. We can make a great intellectual society, or produce circuses if we want to. We have our choice. The intellectual should not be weeping; he should be planning."

But not all intellectuals are so confident, least of all, as was to be apparent later, the scholar most quoted by *Time* in its celebration of the "reconciliation." Barzun, who has inherited the Gallic clarity of his fathers, shudders at the thought of an Athens for the millions. Intellectuals, in his view, have lost their identity. They have no constituency of their own, no unified territory in which the strict standards of the intellect prevail, in which the pulse of logic still beats, in which articulate accuracy reigns. In his cultural critique of the Western world, but especially of the United States (*The House of Intellect*), he cites three spiritual forces as having becoming foes of the intellect: art, science, and philanthropy—by which last he means the foundations which spend millions every year for cultural purposes, but in return put conditions on the intellect. The money of philanthropy, he maintains, should reek of its subject, not of its origin. The clear crystal of alphabet and number, the specific power of the intellect in the Western sense, are threatened; language is devalued and concepts blurred. The unity of knowledge is ruptured as much by the esthetic "creative" confusion of art as by the esoteric aloofness of modern science. There is no communication, any more, among intellectuals. The House of Intellect is traversed by walls of separation. So, says Barzun, "The intellectual class, which ought always to remain independent, even of intellect, has been captivated by art, overawed by science and seduced by philanthropy."

The literary success barometer of recent times has shown that those authors who emphatically assent to the social situation which America has achieved also enjoy the favor of the reading public. Herman Wouk, for instance, followed up his *The Caine Mutiny*—that triumph of military discipline over subversive thought—with *Marjorie Morningstar,* the story of a girl who succumbs to temptation in the person of an unconventional writer, then surmounts her weakness and embraces middle-class respectability. The male counterpart to *Marjorie Morningstar* is Sloan Wilson's *The Man in the Grey Flannel Suit,* a literary eulogy of the new style of life in suburbia adopted by the wealthy upper-middle class. The man in the grey flannel suit finds himself in a not very unusual dilemma involving power, wealth, and prestige on the one hand, and personal happiness on the other. He chooses compromise, and, of course, finds personal happiness in a socially satisfactory framework. Both young novelists, Wouk and Wilson, have become millionaires on the strength of a single book, a quite new species of literary plutocrats, thriving on a geometrical progression of successes procured in turn by book clubs, pocket-book editions, Broadway, Hollywood and television. In his last novel, *Youngblood Hawke,* Herman Wouk even makes this personal situation of the writer the central topic of the book. One critic (in *New Republic*) calls the novel, "a fictional autobiography in cash terms." A writer like Norman Mailer, haunted by the terrible images of the war in the Pacific, must perforce remain on the popular-success sidelines in this game. This does not mean that only those writers achieve success who assent to the social status quo. The exceptions to the rule may be even more significant in highlighting the general trend. As, for instance, *Lolita,* by Nabokov: here is dissent, but of a kind which does not touch the substance or heart of the social situation at all. Social protest in such books is comfortably obscure.

In 1952, the *Partisan Review* published a survey based on what was then the new phenomenon of intellectual conformity to society. Mailer reacted indignantly that he was "in almost total disagreement with the assumptions of this symposium." He found it by no means gratifying that important older novelists like Dos Passos, James T. Farrell, Faulkner, Steinbeck and Hemingway should "have traveled from alienation to varying degrees of acceptance, if not outright proselytizing for the American Century," as the *Partisan Review* had observed.

Such resistance of the artist to reconciliation with society is still—apart from the Beat generation—an isolated phenomenon. For this reconciliation is already much more than mere ideological adjustment; it has led to a structural integration of the intellectual, especially of the poet and novelist, in specific institutions, and this in turn has had quite definite stylistic consequences. As the title of his book indicates, John W. Aldridge, a brilliant young professor of literature, is *In Search of Heresy*. His search has been in vain. The picture he draws is of an institutionalized, intellectual orthodoxy, reflecting a political position of conservative moderation. Aldridge pours bitter scorn on the literati and professors, the critics and their reviews, the cultural foundations and colleges, all indissolubly

linked with one another, forming this new intellectual orthodoxy. Nevertheless, he accepts the process as inevitable. A
vacuum had developed where previously there had been creative protest. Time, as yet, has offered no alternative to this
vacuum but conformity. The values of isolation, of revolt,
have disappeared. The ingenuous struggle against American
"materialism" is no longer possible, and so, the "institutional
values" have interposed themselves on their own: security,
money, power, assent, order, normality.

Novels like Cozzens' *By Love Possessed* or O'Hara's *From
the Terrace* reflect a conservative mood which sees failure, not
progress, as the basic human condition. Published at the end
of the fifties, these novels won wide acclaim; they evidence a
sophisticated, somewhat weary sobering.

A development that is intimately bound up with this mood
is the emergence of an American Alexandrianism, out of the
union of the universities with literary criticism, with writing
as such, with the literary reviews, with the great foundations
which give the money. A change has taken place in the
avant-garde. Instead of the rebellious avant-garde of independent writers and poets, there is an academic avant-garde, orthodox both in its relation to society and in its concepts of style.
Its major contribution in the realm of style is the "New
Criticism," a strictly esthetic, immanent mode of observation,
which has triumphed in the universities over sociological,
psychological, or naturalistic interpretations of literary works.
"Studying the writer's craft"—this has been defined as being
the essence of the New Criticism.

The New Criticism, inspired by Henry James, Ezra Pound,
Eliot and, in Europe, by Croce, was at one time rebellious
too; a revolt against the Marxism of the thirties, a revolt in
particular of the traditionalists of the South. Now, after its
triumph, it is wonderfully suited to be the intellectual guiding
principle of a new orthodoxy. The leading critics are products
of this school of criticism. They are also editors of authorita-

tive literary reviews—university publications like the *Kenyon Review,* the *Sewanee Review,* the *Yale Review,* and *Virginia Quarterly*—and as such are makers or breakers of literary fame. Their dean, John Crowe Ransom, started the movement in 1922, when he, together with Allen Tate, founded the periodical, *The Fugitive.* Francis Fergusson, Cleanth Brooks, Richard Blackmur, Robert Penn Warren and others, who hold literary power as critics, editors, university teachers, dispensers of patronage and authors in their own right, are all adherents of the formalistic school of literary criticism, which weighs a work only in terms of itself, by means of textual interpretation and comparison, and not in terms of anything extraneous to the text. "Close reading" of texts was, first of all, a corrective of romanticism. It has developed analytical disciplines, from which more sociologically or psychoanalytically oriented critics (such as Lionel Trilling) have also profited.

As a "practical estheticism," this approach is better suited than any other to make writing a subject that can be taught and learned, to make literary ability transferable, "to create synthetic James Joyces." It has established "creative writing" as a course in the curriculum, based on the unity of the professor, critic and writer. The writer-*cum*-professor is now a typical figure among American intellectuals. But whereas poets and novelists of repute who now teach at universities—like W. H. Auden, Peter Viereck, Randall Jarrell, John Ciardi, Saul Bellow, Wallace Stegner, and John Cheever—only accepted their posts in the course of their literary careers, it is characteristic of the younger generation of authors that they took "creative writing" courses in the academic institutions and then remained there as teachers of the same subject.

The names of these "university writers" are not as well known in Europe as those of more independent writers like Norman Mailer or James Jones, but they virtually monopolize the pages of the exclusive literary reviews; names such as Saul

Bellow, Elizabeth Hardwick, Flannery O'Connor, Katherine Anne Porter, Robie Macauley, and Edmund Fuller.

Intellectual orthodoxy has received an influential accretion in the shape of the formerly "liberal," or leftist *Partisan Review,* which is independent of the universities, but distributes stipends from foundations such as the Rockefeller Foundation. The way the clever members of this New York literary circle have effected their reconciliation with American society makes the frustrated heresy-hunter, Professor Aldridge, particularly bitter. Here we see serious literary figures, he says, anxiously taking shelter behind the new American mother symbol of egalitarian mass culture. A critic of the *Partisan Review* circle, Leslie Fiedler, sees the history of the American novel as a chain of disguised adolescent homosexuality, emerging now in a new "maturity." But Aldridge sees in this kind of "maturity" only that orthodox values of social conformity have triumphed over the potentially disturbing values of the creative life. This, precisely, is the general tendency. "I assume the institutionalization of the intellectual in America today to be an accomplished fact," writes Aldridge (himself a professor). "Because [the intellectual] could no longer love communism or the elite culture of Europe, he began to love democracy and the mass culture of America, and as anything less than total commitment was unthinkable to him, he felt obliged to love everything about America: equal rights, mass production, mass education, free enterprise, television, supermarkets, used cars, baseball games . . ."

But the position of American intellectuals is not really as hopeless as the temperamental scholar depicts it. The integration of the intellectual in society holds obvious dangers for the creative process, but it had to take place some time, if only because on the other side it takes place by quite different, totalitarian means.

So far, we have dealt with only the literary intellectuals, as the avant-garde of the creative mind in its relationship with society. But much of the conflict between thought and action, which Merle Curti has called the American paradox, may have been relatively resolved by President Kennedy's inclusion of a number of intellectuals from the great universities in government. This is different than the "brain trust" of Franklin Roosevelt. This time, the intellectuals have been integrated in the daily workings of government, with their own responsibilities. They are not mere "experts." While it is true that the questions of politics, particularly in the domestic field, are decided by the President and his inner circle, it is the intellectuals who form the "new style" which has become so characteristic of the Kennedy Administration. This is particularly apparent in the brave attempt to control political decisions, especially in foreign policy, by a cool, anticipatory planning intelligence, at least as far as the elementary forces which rule the world of power politics will permit of such an approach.

Many liberals seem to have expected more from the political elevation of their colleagues. What they forget is that the influence of the intellectuals with whom Kennedy has surrounded himself is in direct relation to their chief's freedom of action. To the extent that this presently somewhat narrow field can be broadened over the years—after Kennedy has successfully dealt with the legacy of unresolved crises that was bequeathed to him—the influence of the intellectual planners and advisers will be able to unfold. It is hardly their fault that their magic touch is not really visible. It is the fault of the circumstances, and these can change.

If there is disenchantment among the liberal intellectuals outside the government, it is not because the President is not "intellectual" enough for them. On the contrary, the obvious intelligence, the absence of the customary clichés, the unconventional mastery with which Kennedy dismisses prejudices deep-rooted in the American tradition, particularly in the tradition of the business world—all these traits appear to have won favor with intellectuals everywhere. The doubts are of another sort. Is the intellectual element in Kennedy and his entourage the result of conviction, of belief in the things of the mind, or only of the realization that the intellect is an indispensable tool of managerial technique in the government of so complex a society?

This question takes the form of a conflict between "pragmatism" and "statesmanship." Many liberal intellectuals believe the Kennedy Administration too pragmatic, or too "political," by which they mean too cautious in questions such as civil rights or the liquidation of unemployment. But such disenchantment overlooks the fact that responsible politics is always the art of the *possible*. Few intellectuals, therefore, would agree with Alfred Kazin, the literary critic, when he says: "Kennedy's shrewd awareness of what intellectuals can do . . . is irrelevant to the tragic issues and contributes nothing to their solution." David Riesman's measured words, speaking for the "liberal left," are fairer: "We wish the Administration well . . . We are critical, but we are not alienated."

If liberals ceased to be critical they would cease to be liberals. But what is historically important is that intellectuals are now "in," inside the little circle that makes history. This may be the height of their reconciliation with American society.

5.

The Deification of Society

EVEN before the Russians—instead of the Americans—had ushered in the planetary age, Dr. Paul Tillich, the philosopher of religion, had said that if the universities should lose their function of seeking truth without compromise, if they should be transformed by an industrial society into research laboratories for industrial purposes, then industrial development itself would come to a standstill. That, he warned, was the danger for America.

The Russian breakthrough in space has brought Tillich's dictum home to the national consciousness as nothing else could have done. An invisible link exists between the search for truth, however abstract this process may be, and power—the industrial, technological power on which the outcome of the world contest largely depends.

America must now part with the deep-rooted myth that a free, democratic society, American society in particular, has, as it were, a built-in mechanism which makes it automatically superior to a Communist society. Now it suddenly appears that a totalitarian society can open to its scientists specific, precisely limited areas of pure research for the purpose of discovering the truth, and that precisely because freedom is lacking in other areas, the best minds are attracted to these zones of scientific freedom.

The sputniks precipitated a merciless reappraisal of the nature of American education, and its relation to the scientific spirit altogether. The misgivings underlying this reappraisal touch bedrock; for the American hierarchy of values is based on education; education is synonymous with the values in which the American most forcibly affirms himself—democracy, freedom, individualism. Only through education do these values become socially operative.

In a civilization which believes in a universal feasibility, even in the feasibility of refashioning the individual, the word "education" has a magic ring. If the whole system of education is called in question, that can mean nothing less than that there is a fundamental flaw in the way of life. It means that the nation as a whole has developed in a manner which bodes ill for its survival, at least as the leading World Power.

Hence, if the possibility looms—and it has had to be conceded even in the highest quarters—that the United States can be beaten by the Soviet Union in certain domains of military technology in the sixties, it is as though the Greeks at the height of their glory had learned that others possessed better philosophers, or the Romans, that others possessed better commanders and governors. The wound cuts deep, but the will to recovery is equally strong. Nevertheless, recovery is rendered more difficult because the patient not only has to treat this one wound, but also has to change some of his most important traits, but without losing his identity. For this, in turn, would be to throw in his hand in advance.

More is involved, therefore, in the crisis in American education than curricula, or the relation of the sciences to the arts, or the threatened submergence of the universities by the technological and scientific faculties. The American colleges are still very far from being thus submerged, for with their thirty thousand new engineers a year they are outstripped both by the Russians with fifty thousand and by the demand in their own country. But it is not the contest in training engineers and technicians that disturbs America so much, for this is a mere matter of adjustment which can easily arise and can also be dealt with satisfactorily. The real difficulties of American higher education lie much deeper.

In the face of these difficulties, arts and sciences are allied. Who, then, is the enemy? The enemy can be identified as the industrial or egalitarian society, or, with Walter Lippmann, as the "Jacobin" democracy, or even as the free society. Whatever its name, it is the social element, the dominant element in American life. This is the force that has subjected education, that has transformed schools and colleges from within.

Every nation has its distinctive genius. The American genius appears to be of an industrial and technological order, yet it is indissolubly linked with the way of life which the continent has developed. The specific achievement of American civilization is rightly considered to be the society which has developed here in the course of three hundred and fifty years, a society where freedom is secured by the neutralizing of power, a society characterized by staggering productivity, increasing classlessness, exciting mobility.

This society, in the American consciousness, has taken on a virtually divine role. Society, not technology, is the true power. Society tolerates no absolute values beside itself, such as truth or knowledge as ends in themselves. And it is a society which panders to the individual, not a society directed to the public interest.

The question arises, what has this almighty society done with the arts and sciences? It will soon become apparent that it has treated them both equally badly, and that therefore the immediate reaction to the sputniks—"More engineers! More scientists!"—did not touch the heart of the education crisis. For what is really at issue is quality and standards. The crisis was, in fact, precipitated by the sudden discovery that in the space of thirty years the Soviets had built up a system of education from scratch, and that that system could produce superior results in scholarship and research in certain fields which, if limited, were nevertheless vital in the power contest between the two great empires. Was America, then, according to the law of "adjustment through competition," to adopt the Soviet educational ideal? Should America deliberately foster a technological elite?

The American answer was "no," and it is characteristic that education should be regarded so emphatically as the unmistakable expression of American society. The patient does not want to lose his identity. The liberal arts must be brought into the closest association with the form of society that is at stake today. On no account should Soviet education be imitated in the priority it gives to the sciences. In view of this position, which is shared by most university teachers and educators, it is the more surprising that there should be so evident a decline in the arts in the institutions of higher learning. Yet the arts have certainly not lost ground to the sciences. The question is so involved that we must first clarify certain terms.

The term "arts" covers, first, the humanities, including sociology, political science and economic theory. The humanities also include languages and the fine arts. Together with the natural sciences, the humanities and social studies constitute the group of theoretical studies (as distinct from applied knowledge) which, under the generic title of liberal arts, were the foundation of the original American college. This gives us a key to the question which faces us here. The situation is quite different in the much more specialized university tradition of continental Europe.

The liberal arts preserved a unity of higher education which covered both arts and sciences; and the fact that "liberal" comes from the Latin "liber"—free—is an important argument in favor of this unity. The American system of higher education is conscious of its origins, which go straight back to the medieval universities of Bologna and Paris. Oxford was founded, in 1170, by a group of scholars from Paris, Cambridge, by a migration from Oxford in 1209; Harvard, in 1636, by a group of learned settlers from Cambridge (just one generation after the first settlers in the wilderness) and Yale, in 1701, by a group from Harvard. Princeton followed in 1746, Columbia in 1754, and the University of Pennsylvania in 1755, to name the oldest foundations.

In essence, their curricula were derived from the medieval liberal arts, from the unity of grammar, rhetoric, logic, mathematics, astronomy and music. These developed into the modern philology, history, philosophy, literature, mathematics, chemistry, physics, the fine arts and social studies, but the unity remained. That unity is still the basis of the curricula of the liberal arts college; it is closely bound up with American society's concept of itself, even though, as we shall see, that society has seriously damaged it.

But, even at the beginning, the humanist tradition and American society made strange bedfellows. For the seventeenth-century Puritan, the purpose of education was to produce the "educated gentleman," as nurtured by Oxford and Cambridge. But the New World would have none of this ideal, though it adopted the educational tradition of the English universities. Just as elementary schools were not to be divided into "popular" and "higher"—with no small consequences for the university—so there was to be no cultivation of a special educated class through the university.

For Jefferson, education was the fulfillment of popular sovereignty, the road to equality of opportunity, the most legitimate vehicle of democratic self-government. But he also regarded what he called the natural aristocracy of talent as the ideal of education. He could not yet realize the inner contradiction in this ideal of education, the contradiction between quality and number, which two hundred years later was to thrust up into the university system from below, with explosive force.

What it means to try to make cultivated gentlemen of a whole people and not, as in England, of a small ruling class, has only become apparent in the twentieth century, and really only since about 1950. Society, that quasi-divine power in American life, has resolved the insoluble problem of scientific humanism for the masses in its own way: it has bypassed it, it has simply ignored it, as the defenders of pure scholarship, whether in the arts or in the sciences, now realize to their horror.

Some forty years ago, even before the pressure of the masses on educational standards became apparent, the pressure of society had already made its imprint on educational methods. It came, as we have said, from below, from the school. It would indeed have been surprising if the American experiment had not set its stamp on education. John Dewey, the philosopher of pragmatism, founded the "progressive" method of education, in opposition to the humanist tradition. But in Europe, too, education has become more pragmatic, the experimental method has been introduced, teaching has been directed away from the traditional content of knowledge to the practical, and the child, as a human being, has been set above the content. But nowhere have the psychological and sociological approaches to education been carried so far as in America.

Dewey's teachings, as practiced by his disciples, have disrupted classroom discipline, inflated curricula with themes of "social adjustment" at the expense of the traditional subject matter, justified an almost anarchic freedom of choice of subjects (compensated for in college by a compulsory lecture program), and, through the points system, equated mathematics with "coeducational cooking," medieval history with fashion, etiquette, or interior decoration, physics with marriage counseling, and so on, since each subject provides equivalent points.

This kind of education, however, had a definite social function at the time of its inception. The great streams of immigrants, millions of children of barely assimilated parents, had to be fashioned into American citizens as quickly as possible.

Neither familiarity with Shakespearean drama nor a knowledge of physics formulae could achieve this end. It was also necessary for the children to learn social modes of behavior, agreeable manners, and the rules of civic life in the American community. Society came first; the child was not educated but "adjusted," a task beyond the powers of the newly arrived parents. Today, immigration is negligible, but the school is still geared to the earlier set of needs.

The theoretical sciences have suffered from this situation almost as much as the arts. Admiral Rickover, the atomic scientist, wrote in 1962: "The Russian school system outproduces the American school system in scientists, linguists, and many times over in technicians of all types."

Inevitably, this situation spills over into the university (the first two years of the American college are comparable to the last two years of the European high school). On this subject Admiral Rickover, who was the architect of the atomic submarine, wrote, in 1958, that in relation to the size of the population and the numbers attending universities, the Soviet Union was producing twice as many technicians and engineers as America. And he made this significant comment, that the Soviet Union had been more realistic in matters of education than the United States, and less fettered by political dogma, however strange that might seem.

After some experiments in the first decade of the revolution, the Soviet Union returned to what American educationists call the authoritarian, class-bound European education system of the nineteenth century. Even after the traumatic shock of the sputniks, Americans do not want to follow the Soviet example.

Columbia University, for instance, does not want to sacrifice the humanist ideal even for the sake of producing more engineers. The faculty believes, so one report states, that a liberal arts education is the best preparation for a creative and responsible career in any domain, including that of engineering.

In recommendations drafted after the initial Soviet achievements in space, the National Education Association exposed the crisis in American schools—overcrowded classrooms, underpaid, badly trained teachers, arbitrary curricula. At the same time it flatly rejected any imitation of Soviet educational methods: "Soviet educational practices cannot be used to achieve American objectives. Soviet education is designed to serve the Communist State. It creates an intellectual and technological elite which wields power and controls opinion in the nation . . . The educational tradition in the United States is totally different. American schools have sought the development of each individual and have avoided the creation of an aristocratic class. Americans have sought to develop leadership and high talent within the framework of the whole society rather than by segregating the most promising."

Here we have the exact reverse of the Soviet position. The Communist State wants an elite. In the free American democracy, on the other hand, education is so much the handmaid of society, it is so completely dependent upon it, that the gifted are not afforded any special opportunities. Yet had not Jefferson postulated a natural aristocracy of talent? It is in this connection that the first reforms have been undertaken. They concern the position of the intellectually superior individual in a society which is both egalitarian and free. "Egalitarian" means that the same opportunities are available to all; it is the principle underlying the experiment of providing high-school education for all, without prior selection on the basis of performance. And "free" means that there can be no commanding of talent by the State. The result is that all pedagogical thinking has centered around the average or even under-average child, for on these depended the success or failure of the gigantic undertaking. The gifted would be able to fend for themselves.

The Rockefeller report, entitled *The Pursuit of Excellence,* rightly states: "We have heaped upon our educators one of the most heroic assignments a society could have invented." But in the process of realizing it, there developed an un-expected and long-hidden form of inequality. It was simply not true that the gifted could fend for themselves. The re-markable discovery was made that certain bad students sud-denly became the best students when they went to schools with more exacting standards. The secret war between equal-ity and quality came into the open. But in the meantime, since the sputnik shock, there has been no meeting of teachers and educators which has not concerned itself with the gifted child. The Department of Health, Education and Welfare has issued recommendations to all school boards on ways of promoting the selection of the gifted; a mass of literature on the subject has emerged.

On the other hand, American society is determined to keep its hold on fundamentals; if there has to be selection, because America has been drawn into a mortal struggle hinging on scientific knowledge, that selection must not engender any class distinctions. The European system of making higher education accessible only to a minority is rejected. The method of selecting among the young must be generous, gracious to the majority, not hard or mechanical.

Thus, what is now being attempted—and it is already under way in about one-fourth of all schools—may be described as a selection process of the gifted that operates as painlessly as possible; painless for the majority of the average students, and painless for the gifted in the sense that they are guarded against the temptation to constitute themselves into a separate and arrogant caste.

The methods used to give special status to the talented begin with "identification" on the fourteen-year level. By means of intelligence tests, ratings and penetrating psychological ob-servation, children are picked out who deserve to receive greater educational opportunities without being separated from the society of their contemporaries. To this end, students receive special counseling from their teachers—hitherto teachers had attended only to the less gifted, who needed protection—and considerable latitude is given them in the choice of subjects, somewhat as in the European university.

Then different possibilities are available to the gifted. There is the program of "enriching" the otherwise unaltered class. This involves group studies in which both gifted and others participate together. Fourteen-year-olds work on such themes, for instance, as "how machines have changed the world" or "how to understand myself and others." These are week-long projects, involving material drawn from outside the school, statistics or Press reports (youngsters travel and interview). The idea is to give the gifted children opportunities for leadership and development. There are also special classes for the gifted, but preferably only in particular subjects, so as not to disrupt their links with the others.

Finally, there are two methods designed to accelerate the education process so that bright youngsters will not be frustrated by the slow, average pace of learning. One is the introduction of college courses in the school, which will later be counted to the student's credit; the other is the admission of students to college before the usual age. Twelve universities, including Yale, Columbia and Chicago, now take students one or two years before the end of school if they show evidence of particular talent. The laborious analysis of Soviet successes has revealed a truth long lost to view: qualities may be latent in difficult, sensitive, shy, "unpopular" children which even an egalitarian democracy cannot afford to ignore.

Americans, then, will not imitate the Russians in the unilateral priority they assign to the sciences and technology. More engineers are being trained, basic research is receiving greater encouragement, and much more money is available for space projects, but the educational reappraisal has taken another turn.

Even the American technologist par excellence, Dr. Killian, who was summoned to the White House on several occasions after the sputniks had been put into orbit, warned of the dangers of over-specialization. Americans, he said, should not imitate their opponents. They should not engage in an academic numbers race with the Soviets. They should not let the pressure in favor of the sciences and engineering destroy the cultivation of first-class talent in other fields. Although Dr. Killian is the head of the greatest technological teaching and research institution in the country, he wants America to have a "humanist culture."

In America, as everywhere in the industrial age, the humanist heritage in the form of the pursuit of pure science is imperiled, but it may be disconcerting for Europeans to find that humanism has more champions here than on their own continent. The President of Yale University, Dr. A. Whitney Griswold, after returning from Europe a few years ago, sadly noted: "A brief educational pilgrimage to Britain, Western Germany and France last summer soon convinced me that we could no longer count on those countries to keep alive the pure flame of liberal learning they lighted eight centuries ago."

To the discerning, the liberal arts, and in particular the humanities, are indispensable to the American way of life. And even if these studies are pursued with a view to serving "democracy" or a "free society" rather than for their own sake, that very fact offers a hope for the humanities such as does not exist in less proudly free societies. Dr. Griswold, in this connection, says: "It follows, does it not, that the freer the society, the greater the responsibilities it imposes upon the individual citizen, and the greater these responsibilities, the greater that citizen's need for the help of the liberal arts."

A Harvard committee report defends the liberal arts, under

the heading of "general education," on the following grounds: a general education underlines the value of the human person in the western tradition, as nurtured by the Greek, Jewish, and Christian cultures; it provides standards of conduct; it insures that all, and not just a chosen few, shall have a well-rounded education; it inculcates the art of being a free man and a citizen, since there can be no political freedom without inner freedom, and no inner freedom without knowledge.

The motive most often cited in defense of what was once an aristocratic education aimed at producing "cultivated gentlemen" is that it promotes a knowledge of the "western tradition" and an understanding of the "value of the individual." A free democracy, so the argument goes, cannot subsist without cultivated human beings. Inevitably, the defender of the arts for the masses—"Why Shakespeare rather than comics?"—looks for arguments of social usefulness.

James B. Conant, one of the leading advocates of educational reform after leaving his post as ambassador to Bonn, speaks of the role of the humanities in the fluid democratic society of a highly industrialized nation. Why, he asks, should a boy who will later be a truck driver, a machinist, a shoe salesman, or a farmer—all of whom attend high school—read the English classics? A foreman, after all, would not do his job better for being familiar with Elizabethan drama, and there would seem to be little point in persuading him to study the subject. The solution for Conant lies again in society. The machinist or the farmer as such do not need the classics, but they are also American citizens, and as citizens they have to find their way about in a highly complex, mobile, composite civilization.

Dr. Conant says of the comprehensive high school, attended by practically the entire youthful population of a community, that it is a uniquely American institution of this century. A school so prodigiously mixed, not only ethnically or racially, but also in respect to class and talent, is a microcosm of adult society. The American school as an institution has far stronger social roots. It is far more strongly integrated in the community than the European school, which depends directly on a central ministry of education. The 140,000 public schools are closely supervised by tens of thousands of school boards, whose members are elected from among the citizens of the rural or municipal communities. Almost as powerful are the parent-teacher associations, in which parents are extremely active in molding the instruction the school provides.

Society, not government, is the master. The school-child learns quite early to think in sociological terms such as family structure, group and individual, democratic consensus, neighborliness, state, village, district, social values. He studies the unions, the business world, population questions, criminology, the play of internal political forces. The average American school-child learns much more about all this than his European contemporary, which explains why most Americans have a far greater knowledge of the multi-tiered functioning of their own society than would seem to correspond to their very modest knowledge of geography. But does this sociological mass education, through the school system, achieve its aim— to produce thinking adherents of a freedom-loving system?

Education for democracy is burdened by an inner dichotomy. It is supposed to educate loyal supporters of the democratic system, but if it is not to be untrue to itself it must also encourage the spirit of criticism which belongs to the free play of forces in a democracy. It must both require the pledge of allegiance to the flag, with which every American child starts the school day, and encourage the use of the basic right of free opinion. There is no doubt that the inculcation of civic loyalty, of some degree of American nationalism, is given far greater encouragement than the other aspect of democracy, critical thought. The "democratic" structure of local school boards of elected citizens, in which the biggest taxpayers often predominate, easily leads to a situation where teachers are taken to task for permitting a frank discussion of controversial issues. The dichotomy has not yet been resolved.

A number of educators believe that the essence of the crisis in education lies in the weak position of teachers, who are overwhelmingly of the female sex. Teachers have become dependent tools of committees in which politicians hardly allow them to have new or independent ideas, even inside the classroom.

All the writing in defense of the liberal arts, with emphasis on the avoidance of professional specialization, would be unnecessary if the "democratization of the cultivated gentleman" had not proved highly dangerous.

America today is the only nation in the world where the liberal arts, in the humanist and medieval sense, can be a constituent element of political conviction. At the same time, the arts and, hardly less, the theoretical sciences are being increasingly driven to the fringes of higher education, they attract an ever decreasing proportion of students, and knowledge of the humanist tradition—in fact, knowledge altogether—is becoming increasingly limited.

The enemy of the arts is not the sciences, or vice versa; they have no enemy in America. But the halls of learning have been taken over by an egalitarian society, and commandeered for purposes which, though they may borrow the luster of great universities, from their liberal arts, have very little else in common with them.

Some sixty per cent of America's youth—twelve million—attend high school. Of these, one-third go on to colleges and universities, as against one-twentieth in Europe. In 1962, four million students attended two thousand institutions of higher learning. By 1970, the number is expected to rise to seven million. Two-thirds of all American colleges are privately endowed. Most are colleges which go no further than the Bachelor of Arts degree (which has no equivalent in continental European universities, but corresponds to the fourth semester of their *Studium Generale*). The American Masters degree corresponds, more or less, to the European professional degree (called "diploma"), although the requirements are usually somewhat higher for the European degree.

The American Doctor of Philosophy degree is approximately equal to the European doctorate in the humanities, especially since the thesis time in the United States has been shortened recently, in the bigger universities, such as Columbia and Harvard. Formerly, the time required was disproportionately long (sometimes up to twelve years) and, consequently, the Ph.D. program was less-often taken. Now, with shortened time requirements, more students are taking doctoral programs. There are no strict academic standards in the United States; quality varies from the most academically select universities in the world (like Princeton, or Harvard) to small, often sub-average colleges.

The tremendous population rise since the forties (the American population is increasing at the rate of some three million annually) has turned into an explosive force the egalitarian principle, that if possible everyone should go to college and as many as possible to university. The requirements of society have burst open the colleges and universities not only in a physical sense but also as regards their curricula. It is not the increasing importance of technology in the modern world that has edged out the liberal arts tradition. That would imply that within the academic disciplines the balance had shifted to scientific work. What has really happened is a kind of quiet seizure of power by industry and commerce within the academic world.

Surveys such as William H. Whyte, for instance, uses in his *The Organization Man,* show that the American business and technical schools which have developed during the past hundred years lure an increasing number (even of gifted students) away from the liberal arts colleges. The schools in question are primarily business, agricultural and engineering colleges. Not only have additional numbers streamed into these specialized schools, but also the arts and science departments have not been able to maintain their existing enrollments.

Only a small minority of students still take degrees in the traditional disciplines; the sciences have suffered from this exodus no less than the arts. Many who would formerly have studied history, economics or sociology, to prepare themselves for an executive career in big business, now go to business schools. Many who would formerly have studied science or mathematics now go to engineering or technical schools. The conflict, as Whyte puts it, is not between the humanities and the sciences, but between pure and applied knowledge. Moreover, the enrollment even of the engineering schools is topped by that of the business schools; the latter, incidentally, go so far as to give degrees in "public relations."

To cite some available figures: In the 1954-55 class of college graduates the biggest single group was "business," accounting for 19.4 per cent of the total. All the graduates in mathematics, physics, biology, the social sciences and the arts, taken together, accounted for only 26.6 per cent of the total. Engineering accounted for 12.3 per cent; teaching (teachers are trained in educational technique and hardly at all in the other branches of learning), 8.1 per cent; agriculture, 3.8 per cent. The balance was accounted for by law, theology and medicine.

There is a shortage in America not only of doctors and lawyers, chemists and psychologists, but also of engineers. The ravenous appetite of the giant industrial bureaucracies for academic progeny, however laudable it may be in itself, has upset the internal balance of the university.

The reason for the astonishing shortage of technologists is not that students have migrated into the "ivory tower" of pure knowledge, as the foes of the "medieval" arts or the "warmed-up Renaissance" maintain, but that the streams of new students are directed through academic channels into the great firms, which even send their recruiting agents to the campuses to get college graduates to commit themselves before they leave the academic world. It is clear that in this intimate welding of university and industry, which spares the young graduate even the need to look for his first job, the least risky procedure for the personnel department of a firm is not to give preference to pure research students, however much the economists at the top may esteem the need for a "well-rounded" general education for business leadership.

In the major American universities and some technical schools there has been, for some time, a counter-movement to revive the humanities even in the industrial world which has flooded the university. But the great majority of educational institutions still follow the trend toward "practical" instruction, toward over-specialization in the service of a competitive industrial society. The arts—and this applies no less to basic research in science and mathematics—seem to be fighting a rearguard action in the universities; for the pressure of numbers also generates increased costs. Since the principle of private endowment should not and cannot be abandoned, this means that the rich and powerful corporations are increasingly becoming the patrons of the universities and colleges. It would need almost superhuman insight on the part of these firms to dedicate themselves to salvaging the arts, although among the older generation of business leaders there still exists a sense of responsibility in this direction. Their younger successors, however, are already products of the business schools.

So the chain of cause and effect progresses. An egalitarian society wants to make cultivated gentlemen of all; it regards the humanist tradition as indispensable to its free way of life; by allowing the masses to pour into the high schools and then into the colleges, it opens the academic world to precisely this society which has become increasingly pleasure-seeking, intoxicated with consumer goods, inconceivably productive and prosperous. It has therefore fashioned the educational world according to its own desires, and the discovery was bound to be made one day that the ideal of education was no longer the cultivated gentleman, but the socially adjusted young executive, psychologically equipped for leadership and group relations, in tune with society, scientifically trained in the techniques of industrial management, distribution, sales and publicity. The Greek has turned Carthaginian.

To the outside world, America often appears as a nation of technicians, as a technocracy whose dynamism is fed by ever-new inventions, from the Model-T to the electronic, and now the atomic, devices which are revolutionizing the material world. Nevertheless, the place of honor in the social hierarchy goes not to the technician, nor even to the research scientist who discovers the formulae, but to industry: to the executives, distributors, salesmen, advertisers, even, as in the automobile industry, to the "stylists." Anthropologists, questioning school-children, have found a prejudice against science. The scientist in his laboratory is regarded as asocial, godless, introverted, exposed to dangers and suspicions, a man of pure reason, unsporting, possessed by ideas—in short, abnormal.

This has changed, however, since the first American orbited in space. Astronaut Glenn has made youth space-conscious. And space means science and engineering. A representative of the Space Administration says: "As we look ahead, our most critical need seems to be for engineer-scientists, for engineering Ph.D.'s."

The extent of the influence of the new space age on American education will not be known for some years to come. Thus far, it is still true that the scientific spirit has subordinated itself to the needs of society. Is this endemic in the American character or only the accidental result of a socio-economic development? The untheoretical, pragmatic spirit is rooted in the American experience and colors its practice. Max Lerner writes in *America as a Civilization:* "America is a civilization founded on science and rooted in its achievements. Without science the whole ribbed frame of American technology, and with it American power, would have been impossible . . . The whole atmosphere surrounding the settlement and peopling of America was an atmosphere of scientific beginnings . . ." But the tremendous achievements of the scientific spirit of Americans were always, as was almost inevitable from the nature of their experiment in living, less in the realm of pure than of applied science.

The United States has produced only two theoreticians of international significance—the physicist, Willard Gibbs, and the epistemologist, Charles S. Peirce—but it has produced innumerable inventors and technological pioneers. Since 1945, the United States has won more Nobel prizes than any other country. And in the field of theoretical physics, chemistry, biology and mathematics, too, the United States possesses university faculties of high caliber, superior to those of the Old World. This is in no small measure a result of politically induced immigration. But even in the field of atomic science, the specifically American contribution has always been the combination of experimental science with economic organization, the dynamic translation of formulae into energy, speed, movement. This pragmatism originally did not exclude genuine scientific search for truth as an end in itself, the faculty of pure wonder, "idle curiosity," as the impetus to research. But this attitude is today largely stifled by two structural changes in the scientific world: first, the removal of research to the giant laboratories of industry, which have become the *Maecenae* of the sciences, but also their strict employers; secondly, the militarization of physics, chemistry and biology.

When technology delivers the new weapons, this scientific work itself becomes a part of national defense, and compulsory secrecy spreads its pall over free research. There is little to attract a scholarly temperament in the prospect of fitting into an industrial team or a military administrative bureaucracy.

That is what the struggle with the Soviet Union has brought home to responsible Americans. If the realization bears fruit, it will be just as beneficial to the liberal arts as to basic scientific research. America has rediscovered that even from the most empirical of all viewpoints—that of power and international position based on power—the disinterested questioning and seeking, the intellectual curiosity, the independent reflection of the solitary (perhaps even asocial) thinker are not to be despised or the society will one day discover that its roots are withering away. This, of course, is a matter of the intellectual climate of the country, of the hierarchy of social values, and therefore not something that can be effected by a mechanical changeover or by the vast sums that are now flowing into basic research. The change must first take place in the national ethos, and it seems that it has already been recognized as at least necessary.

Robert Oppenheimer, who is a humanist as well as a nuclear physicist, states the problem facing the American nation at the present time in much the same way as his academic colleague, Jacques Barzun. In an essay he wrote even before the Russian success in space, but already in connection with the scientific contest with the Soviet Union, Oppenheimer said: "What we need is a vastly greater intellectual vigor and discipline; a more habitual and widespread openmindedness; and a kind of indefatigability . . . It is not true that our land is poor in curiosity, in true learning, in the habit of smelling out one's own self-delusion. There is respect for learning and for expertness, and a proper recognition of the role of ignorance; but of none of these is there enough, either among us, or in the value with which they are held by us, if indeed government by the people is not to perish."

In other words, the patient need not lose his personality, but he should have more of one element and less of the other. He must therefore correct his hierarchy of values; he must not elevate human society to the rank of the divine; he must recognize values which transcend society.

But is this not taking place in the religious revival, in the renewal of the Christian faith, for which the churches cite such impressive figures? Even among intellectuals, of the generations following Sinclair Lewis, it has become old-fashioned to be anti-clerical. But does "*not* being anti-God" mean "being *for* God"? How is this great paradox to be explained, that the churches are ever fuller, the contributions for their support ever larger, endeavors to acquire religious knowledge ever more widespread, while at the same time society is becoming ever more worldly, ever more uninhibitedly earthy in the sense of a "Carthaginian" pleasure-seeking, ever farther removed from the innerworldly asceticism of early American Calvinism?

Theologians are anxiously wondering if the religious revival is not merely a variety of social conformism. The full churches would then be the product of a perhaps unconscious form of social imitation; a consequence of the pressure of neighborhood living in suburbia; an indication that confessions are being enlisted to promote the greater glory of the American way of life. Religion, according to this interpretation, has been inserted in American life, more effectively, certainly, than in the twenties or thirties, but merely inserted, and is in no way dominant, as one would think if there were a real religious reawakening.

The specific question arising in connection with the Christian revival is whether there really can be such a movement so long as the notion of sin is excluded. In a society which approves itself so unquestioningly under the banner of prosperity, the consciousness of sin has largely disappeared. The renewal of the American churches has many positive features at a time when the process of deChristianization has gripped large areas of Europe. But the theologians will one day have to decide whether there can be a Christian reawakening of the masses without a consciousness of sin and grace, without Christian radicalism and what a revival, where all this is lacking, can mean for the Christian religion.

One may ask whether this will lead to a transformation of the Christian religion after the pattern of Chinese Confucianism, which was a directive for the "right" living in society.

6.

The Inner Conflict

IN THE South, one quarter of the nation, there is taking place the great debate between the races, involving much more than the social well-being of nearly fifty million people, white and colored alike. Of all American experiments, this is the most hazardous.

It began, unnoticed, three centuries ago, when the first slave ship from Africa landed in the British colony of Virginia. It has since become the greatest social problem of the United States, overshadowing every other minority problem. Whether and how the colored tenth of the population of this enormous country will be integrated in the structure of society—this is coming to be the test of the fundamental beliefs underlying the American ethos. The racial problem has cost America loss of sympathy in all parts of the world. As one American has put it, "Little Rock is our Algeria."

But for America, the issue is more serious even than that. Its moral unity is jeopardized if a section of the country—a section, moreover, that is most intimately bound up with its birth as a nation—persists in a state of open or concealed revolt against the Federal Government and against the Federal Constitution itself. For that is the peculiar situation of the Deep South, since its white leaders have been contesting the Supreme Court decision of May 17, 1954, ruling that compulsory segregation of the races in the schools was unconstitutional.

The first reaction of the "sovereign" southern states to the decision of the highest legal tribunal—which put an end to a sixty-year era of legal *apartheid*—was organized resistance. Everywhere the first expedient was to bypass the Supreme Court decision by simply closing the entire public school system. White children went to private schools, colored to none. This solution made it possible to keep colored children out of white schools without provoking the mob violence which, in 1957, brought international notoriety to Little Rock, the capital of Arkansas, and created something in the nature of a local state of civil war, when the President sent paratroopers to the scene. (Today, a few Negroes are admitted to the Central High School of Little Rock.)

In contrast with the rural areas, where the poulation is often predominantly Negro, many southern cities saw the emergence of a form of parents' protest against the expedient of closing the public schools. Private schools were expensive; and hastily improvised as they were, they were not as good. The public schools were, for the most part, reopened, and a "token" admission of colored children—a small number in a few schools—was the price paid to the law of the land. Large areas of the South are now sprinkled with these symbolic white-black schools. Some southern states, such as Arkansas, Tennessee, and Texas, resorted to this method soon after the Supreme Court had rendered its decision; they divided themselves into counties which either adopted a limited form of integration, or maintained complete segregation. This unequal compromise, which slowly—very slowly —operated in favor of the Negroes, is now typical of the southern states outside the hard core of resistance, that is, outside South Carolina, Georgia, Alabama, Mississippi and Louisiana. The colored children in "token" schools, mostly over thirteen, in tiny groups of three or four, as against perhaps one thousand whites, pay no small price in terms of courage in a necessarily cruel situation—a real "frontier" situation.

The five northernmost states of the South—Kentucky, Maryland, Missouri, Oklahoma, and West Virginia—as well as the federal capital of Washington, D.C., have abolished segregation and opened the doors of their previously all-white schools to 250,000 Negro children.

In the seventeen southern and border states there are 2,813 school districts where white and colored populations live side by side. Of these districts, 910 were desegregated by 1962. That is, only about one-third. "Desegregated" means, of course, that Negro children are admitted on a token basis.

But the states which waged the war of secession against the North one hundred years ago, have never forgotten what Yankee civilization did to them, and civil war flares up anew from time to time against the "other America." This war is not conducted in the gay-colored uniforms of the nineteenth century, not with the old cannons and fortresses which everywhere in the South are revered as monuments, but by state laws that undermine the federal law, by the resistance of White Citizens' Councils and the revived Ku Klux Klan, by a systematically fostered climate of intolerance and the intimidation of all forces of moderation, by economic pressure in the form of boycott or worse, by the arousing of white mobs whenever this appears opportune, and in extreme cases—rare indeed, but they do occur—by lynching and murder. (In Mississippi, in 1959, a Negro named Parker was charged with the rape of a white woman. He was hauled out of jail and lynched. The perpetrators could never be brought to trial—though their names were known—because their fellow citizens covered up for them.)

White resistance is strongest in the enormous area extending from southern Virginia, on the Atlantic coast, to western Texas, on the Gulf of Mexico. This area is known as the Black Belt, not because the population is predominantly colored (although in some parts Negroes constitute as much as eighty per cent of the population), but because of the rich black soil, in which cotton and tobacco are grown on huge plantations. It was here that the "gracious living" of the planter aristocracy thrived prior to the Civil War, based on a patriarchal form of slavery. This was the "Old South," the only society containing seeds of feudalism in the New World. This incipient feudalism collapsed with the Civil War, but there is no doubt that it left deep traces in the American body politic. The conservative, distinctively "southern" style of living inherited from that regime is felt to be threatened today —as it was a century ago—by the egalitarian North. This is felt to be a mortal threat where, as in large areas of Mississippi, Negroes constitute a majority of the population.

Since the Second World War, after decades of deliberate neglect, the South has made rapid strides towards industrialization with the aid of the capital invested there by powerful East Coast industrial corporations. The plantation economy has therefore lost its paramount position, though this economic development is not reflected in the political sphere. In the Black Belt, voting procedures have remained unchanged since the turn of the century, and a handful of rural voters are entitled to the same representation on the state legislature as some 2,000 city voters. The plantation, then, with its cheap, illiterate and therefore malleable labor force of Negro sharecroppers, has long since ceased to be the principal source of wealth to the South. But the rural areas, whose position on the racial problem and whose economic thinking stem from the lustrous days of the planter aristocracy, from the heritage of lordship and slavery, still possess political control. That is why white resistance to the lifting of segregation is not only tolerated but encouraged by the state governments and legislatures. That is why new state laws are enacted obstructing school integration by representing public schools as private schools, by imposing sanctions on teachers of both races, by withholding public funds and banning the principal Negro organizations—regardless of what the Federal Supreme Court may have decided and ordered.

It is an anguishing situation. The southern states, the oldest cultural stratum of the New World, are making use of the checks and balances provided in the United States Constitution to defend what they regard as their freedom—the freedom to live in accordance with their own standards. They invoke states' rights to oppose the application of another principle of the Constitution—equality—to their territories. Two of the constituent principles of America's political life, equality and freedom, issue in conflict and jeopardize national unity. The southern political leaders are deeply resentful of the federal authorities in Washington for their unwillingness to recognize a freedom based on inequality. But they can console themselves with the reflection that the powers of the central government to intervene through the Department of Justice and the Federal Bureau of Investigation are strictly limited. It is the genius of the American Constitution that it precludes the abuse of power by means of an intricate system of balances. No one, not even the northern "liberals," wants to sacrifice these safeguards.

The authors of the Constitution certainly did not foresee such a conflict. Thomas Jefferson, who drafted the Declaration of Independence, was a great southerner. He was a true representative of the refined, esthetic, southern aristocracy, yet he wrote in the Declaration of Independence that all men are born equal and possessed of inalienable rights. He realized that this principle was inconsistent with the practice of slavery, but he was forced to strike out the phrase in his draft admitting this inconsistency, because some of the "southern gentry" objected to having human dignity so explicitly ascribed to slaves. For them, this could be a satisfactory solution to the contradiction. But equality is as indivisible as peace. The successors of those southern gentry are seeking, by means of a resistance that can only be regarded as a rearguard action, to play off one part of the Constitution against the other. The question is just how long will they succeed in holding up a development which historical experience shows to be irresistible. A few decades mean much to a generation, and in Atlanta, the capital of Georgia, one can hear people say that it will be possible to delay the tearing down of the walls of racial separation for another thirty or forty years.

What the white leaders of the South are attempting is an experiment in isolation, at a time when everywhere in the world there is a growing sense of interdependence. In so doing, they are revealing a situation of quasi-infinite complexity, which began when the first slaves were brought over from Africa to become the unexpected human foundation of a wealth—based on cotton, tobacco, sugar, and rice—which the first settlers had not intended to build up on an aristocratic basis. Indeed, the complexity is so great that it sometimes appears almost hopeless to arrive at the truth.

A few miles from Atlanta, surrounded by old, shady trees, there stand the marble-walled buildings of Emory University, remarkable for the classical simplicity of their architecture. As with all American universities, the campus is a little city unto itself. Here, three thousand students, of both sexes, live and work, and, sometimes, marry. The professors, far more numerous in proportion to the students than in Europe, live in the lovely suburbs of Atlanta, whose architecture breathes the elegance and culture of the old planter aristocracy. The southern style of life is everywhere perceptible. Conservatism is in the very air; a tranquil hush seems to reign over the campus—complete, if the parked cars, almost as numerous as the students within this marble city of learning, were not there to recall the restless mobility of American life (which makes the daily existense of these young people so different from that of their European contemporaries).

What better place could there be to seek information about the terrible problem that haunts the South and tears at the nerves of its population, both white and colored, than here, in the quiet of this Methodist university, in conversation with scholars accustomed to dispassionate observation?

The conflict between white and colored Americans has entered its final stages in the southern states. The Negro population here is over ten million, or nearly two-thirds of all American Negroes. They constitute about one-quarter of the entire population of the southern states, which, in their turn, comprise about one-quarter of the total population of the United States. But these figures reveal nothing of the moral and political significance of what is taking place here between the races. They reveal nothing of the terror exercised by the White Citizens' Councils, the re-emergence of the Ku Klux Klan, white mob action against colored school children, fear and hysteria, economic boycott, and violence.

In the cultivated atmosphere of Emory University, such things seem hardly credible. And, in fact, one hears from learned professors what one is constantly hearing in somewhat cruder form from southerners generally; namely, that the racial conflict is overdramatized by northern observers. It would not exist at all, they maintain, if the South were left alone, if the relationship between white and colored were patriarchally ordered, if the colored intellectual elite did not provoke unrest. Even within this elite, so one is informed, many fear that if separate institutions are abolished, they will lose their jobs—teachers and radio announcers, for instance, and even agitators of the principal activist Negro organization, the National Association for the Advancement of Colored People.

The partisan of the racial status quo, who observes city and rural life in the South, can gather a number of impressions to confirm his philosophy. True, Negroes may not enter white hotels or restaurants; they have to use separate entrances to movies (and washrooms) with the sign "Colored" over them; they may swim—if at all—only at special beaches; standing, they have to drink the Coca-Cola which they buy from the vendor; mixed marriages are severely punished; they have to worship God in separate churches (with a few exceptions); and even death does not unite them with the whites, for funeral homes and cemeteries are also segregated. On the other hand, Negroes can be seen everywhere driving cars that are often expensive; many of them are well dressed (even though most of them seem unimaginably poor, but even in that poverty they betray the lighthearted *joie de vivre* which stems from an inexhaustible vitality). In the South, not only in New York, there are Negroes who have grown rich, who live in beautiful suburbs, among them some who have recently become millionaires, mostly real-estate dealers. Furthermore, despite the racial hostility which has flared up again since 1954, real advances have been made: in Atlanta, for instance, with its population of half a million, where the mayor owes his office in part to the colored vote, sports grounds, swimming pools and public golf courses are accessible to white and colored alike.

Alongside the growing economic power of the Negroes— related to advances in education—alongside the passive resistance inculcated by the churches, there is a third factor which will contribute to the nonviolent, "democratic" integration of colored citizens in the American social structure in the sixties. This is the protection of Negro voting rights as assured by Congress.

Professional associations of doctors, nurses, lawyers, ministers, and teachers are beginning to accept colored members. Nevertheless, strange incongruities occur. For instance, the Pan-American Club of Atlanta gave a dinner at Emory in honor of an English hispanologist. The vice-president of the association of French teachers, whose name the club had found on the membership list, was invited. As she was accepting the invitation on the telephone, she mentioned that she was colored. The invitation was withdrawn. To eat at

the same table seems impossible even if one has long been
able to sit in the same lecture hall.

Another "tablecloth incident" shows how irrational is much
of the attitude of the whites on the racial question. A white
woman had entertained a mixed working committee in her
house. When a friend asked her "since when did she eat at the
same table with Negroes?," she protested: "But I didn't
put any tablecloth on the table!" The horror of close contact
with members of the colored race is most deeply ingrained,
sometimes involuntarily, in the intimate sphere of usage and
manners, in the realm of etiquette.

Passive resistance, nourished by the study of Gandhi's
techniques and previously tried out by Negro churches,
has been employed, since 1960, in the fight for "moral rights."
The first target of passive resistance was the strange rule
of racial etiquette that Negroes wishing to eat at luncheon
counters in department stores must be served standing,
whereas whites sit on high stools. Negro students, showing a
restraint in the face of provocation that their race had not
previously been credited with, staged sit-down strikes at
such counters. They demonstrated, thereby, that they wanted
no more of the sandwiches—especially thickly spread by the
colored kitchen help—at the rear entrance, but that they
wished to sit with the whites at the counter and consume their
more meager portions there. The emergence of Negro students, trained in the methods of passive resistance, to leadership in the racial conflict, is as new as their determination to
oppose the moral nuances of segregation. They regard it as
absurd that a Negro woman should be able to try on lingerie
in a store, after which, if she does not buy it, it is again put
on display, but that in the same store she must drink her
coffee standing. The requirement, writes Harry Golden, that
the Negro should live "vertically" is the last bulwark of the
agrarian ante-bellum South.

White and colored in the deep South have one thing in

common: they know that their problem is endlessly complex and is made up of a thousand individual human situations. Nothing is more inappropriate, or indeed foolish, than to portray the situation in hasty abstractions, in absolute black and white, to use a fitting metaphor. Robert Penn Warren, in his *Inner Conflict in the South,* describes the "irremediable self-division" of the present-day Southerner. He is torn by primitive hate of the "nigger" and torturing doubts about the moral (and historical) tenability of his position. According to the racist metaphysic of the segregationists, Negroes are biologically and inevitably on a lower level than whites, and even the Bible is appropriated to bear the doctrine out: segregation, so it is maintained, is of divine, not human decree. But only the extremist minority have been able to reconcile such beliefs with their Christian conscience.

Southerners who defend the status quo are, perhaps, not wrong when they say that racial tensions are introduced from without. The degree of truth or falsehood of this argument becomes clear when one hears the other side.

The Negro university of Atlanta consists of red brick buildings with high windows, white doors and columns, forming a circle around a huge expanse of grass. Like Emory, this university, financed by private endowments from the North, houses some three thousand students. Oddly enough, one's first impression is that this campus is more European than Emory. The explanation: the absence of the thousands of cars which line all the streets of the Emory campus.

Talking to the sociology professor—who knows so much about Pareto and Max Weber, who uses the German word *"Geist"* to express what is changing in the South despite all obstacles—the theory that the Negroes are content with the status quo, and that discontent is artificially disturbed by the "collectivist" and liberal North, breaks down. Pointing to his face, he said: "That is what makes our problem so conspicuous." For the colored sociologist, the Negro problem is only a particular instance of the eternal American minority problem, of the struggle of immigrant groups—in this case the descendants of immigrants introduced by force—to rise into the American middle class, which increasingly is becoming the only class, although traversed by innumerable "levels."

This applies to Negroes no less than to all others—Poles, Hungarians, Jews, Irish, Chinese, Mexicans, Puerto Ricans, and so on, as well as to the "old stocks," the English and Germans, who came to the country in greater numbers than all the others and yet could still find themselves harassed as minorities. Negroes, said the professor, are very "level-conscious." If the Negro is legally cut off from the rest, he cannot rise within the American middle class. The Negro elite rejects *apartheid* because it necessarily debars the Negro from the opportunities for advancement available to all Americans, however clean the schools may be that are built for colored children. For Negroes, propaganda to the contrary notwithstanding, are passionate Americans. They do not want to be anything else.

Like all Negro intellectuals, the professor of sociology is convinced of the impossibility of cordoning off any part of the world in this day and age. The South, too, has been swept into the movement of interdependence which is knitting the world together. The racial problem, which might have remained dormant in a closed, conservative South, has now been irreversibly posed, never to be returned to obscurity. The professor knows Hegel, and he would agree that the "universal spirit" is on his side. But how rapidly the "universal spirit" will permeate the South even he cannot predict.

When the Supreme Court ruled, in 1954, that segregation in the schools was unconstitutional, the time seemed ripe for dealing with one of the most dangerous sores in the American social system, and this for a number of interconnected reasons. Outside the former slave states, so obviously un-Christian and undemocratic a practice as racial discrimination had long burdened the American conscience. In the war, Negroes had fought and died for their country. Out of considerations of international politics, the White House championed a liberal racial policy at home. And when the Supereme Court announced its decision, that decision was at once used by diplomacy to spread the image of an America free from racial prejudice, among the peoples of Asia and Africa. It was a triumph for America in the ideological debate of the world. Thurgood Marshall, who had represented the Negro case before the Supreme Court, declared afterwards: "This decision gives the lie to Communist propaganda . . . For once, our country can hold its head up, and for that I am eternally grateful. I am grateful, not just as a Negro, but as an American."

One of the main arguments of the Supreme Court judges was that the American Negro's belief in his country's adherence to law and justice should not be disappointed. Here, at least, the struggle for equal rights should be conducted without violence, not as in the territories of the old colonial powers. The Negro elite espoused the cause of nonviolence. And their cause would be lost were they to proceed in any other way. But the same can hardly be said of the white side. There, the Supreme Court ruling had an effect exactly contrary to what had been anticipated. After a period of hesitation, opposition forces built up a movement of resistance led by extremists with determination, reckless demagogy and ample funds. The sociological law of oligarchy—of the leadership of the few in mass movements—was borne out. From total obscurity there suddenly appeared organizers of "White Citizens' Councils," and, in the spirit of intolerance which they bred, even the brutal Ku Klux Klan began to raise its head again, however sporadically, complete with hoods and flaming torches.

The facts, as compiled by a white research group in Atlanta, are these. The movement of the White Citizens' Councils came into being in the Mississippi Delta, following the Supreme Court decision of May, 1954. Leading citizens of Sunflower County met in a secret founding session and adopted the slogan: "Public sentiment is the law." In six weeks, the organization had spread to seventeen neighboring counties. By the end of the year, it was already a powerful movement in Mississippi, Alabama and South Carolina. Since then, White Citizens' Councils have sprung up in all the southern states.

At first, they expected to have to work indirectly, using economic pressure, influencing municipal and state legislation. Using the influence available to leading citizens in rural counties, they would act like a "manicured Ku Klux Klan," with "economic lynch laws," as a southern newspaper wrote at the time. But the citizens' councils have since become a mass movement of intimidation, with a membership of several hundred thousand. Their leaders have ties with the holders of political power in the various states. Often, they themselves are state senators. The movement is increasingly concerned with due process; it can indeed proceed "legally," since it makes the state laws itself, laws abolishing rights already acquired (such as Negro voting rights), and thus laws that clash with federal law.

The citizens' councils want to be "respectable," but in the shadow of their interpretation of the law, all kinds of dubious activity must inevitably thrive, an example being the Ku Klux Klan, which is also anti-Semitic and anti-Catholic. How could it be otherwise, when the Senator from Mississippi, James Eastland, thus expresses himself about the highest judges in the land: "The Supreme Court of the United States, in the false name of law and justice, has perpetrated a monstrous crime. It presents a clear threat and present danger . . . to the foundations of our republican form of government. The antisegregation decisions are dishonest decisions . . . these decisions were dictated by political pressure groups bent upon the destruction of the American form of government, and the mongrelization of the white race. The judges . . . have disgraced the high office which they hold. The court has responded to a radical pro-Communist political movement in this country."

Senator Eastland used what is perhaps the most powerful weapon in the white extremists' arsenal when he spoke of "mongrelization." A state senator in Alabama put it even more graphically when he ascribed to a militant Negro organization the aim of "opening the bedrooms of our white women to colored husbands."

In the Negro press, there are occasional demands for the lifting of the ban on marriages between the races. On this point, some quite radical things may sometimes be said by Negroes too, for extremism is contagious. But the sexual fear motive is quite specifically utilized by segregationists in the fight against desegregated schools. This is not only irrational—and irrationality lies at the heart of the matter—but it is also illogical. Serious observers cite the answer of a student at the University of South Carolina who was asked at a meeting by a speaker of the Ku Klux Klan: "Would you want your sister to marry a Negro?" The student replied: "She can say no, can't she?"

Not only the demagogues of the White Citizens' Councils, but also responsible politicians of the southern states, accuse the Supreme Court of introducing "mongrelization" by its decisions. But the spokesmen of this fear forget that on the Negro side, too, strong forces are at work in favor of keeping a voluntary distance between the races long after the legal barriers—which painfully embody the false dogma of their biological inferiority—have fallen. Actually, up till a hundred years ago, sexual relations between white men and Negro women were not exactly infrequent, as a result of which a "mongrelization" did in fact arise at the time. But of course the offspring of such unions were inevitably regarded as belonging to the Negro race. (However, statistics for 1900 show that each year ten thousand such light-skinned mulattoes secretly crossed the barrier around the white world. This process of "passing" still exists today, on a much smaller scale.)

Even in states where segregation has never been legally enforced, intermarriage has been quite rare. The famous "melting pot" has not really operated within the white race, let alone between peoples of different color. All the more reason to suppose that the deep-rooted barrier between white and colored will be maintained for generations to come. For that matter, if Negroes want to obtain the legal right to attend hitherto all-white schools, that does not necessarily mean that they, in fact, want to send their children there. This applies equally to other areas of racial equality in status.

The Supreme Court did not, after all, as the spokesmen of the White Citizens' Councils maintain, proclaim that the races should be compulsorily brought together, after being compulsorily kept apart. All it did was to give the principle of free choice force of law. There will always be all-Negro schools as long as Negroes live together in large numbers. But Negroes will be able to attend these schools in the knowledge that they do so of their own free will, once the southern states decide to abandon altogether a resistance which violates the Constitution.

On this point the Supreme Court declared in 1954: "To separate them [the children] from others of similar age and qualifications simply because of their race generates a feeling of inferiority as to their status in the community that may affect their hearts and minds in a way unlikely ever to be undone." The judges were cautiously voicing a fear which the white race can justifiably harbor, namely, that a prolonged denial of the constitutional rights of millions of American Negroes could drive them into a position of hostility to the State, a hostility which would then seek oulets.

But the whites who have power and influence in the South and do not allow the moderates to speak are not concerned about that. What they fear is that the Negroes would swarm across the barrier between the races if legal separation were abolished. They overlook the fact that the structures of the separate Negro society have meanwhile developed a considerable *vis inertiae* of their own.

Sociological investigations conducted by the Negro university of Atlanta have shown that, in the Negro communities too, racial pride, economic interest, tradition, emotional inhibitions, and monopolistic considerations place strong brakes on actual, as opposed to formal, integration. A part of the tremendous prosperity of America in the last decade has accrued to the Negroes too, and has developed among them a stratified social order, in which there is a far from unified approach to the racial problem. The urbanization of the southern Negro and the movement of the Negro to the North have led to the slums of many urban centers being taken over by the colored. But, Negroes also populate prosperous suburbs of their own, they own banks, insurance companies, radio stations, and hotels (and in all these enterprises there is often white capital). A kind of "creeping integration" is taking place on the economic level since industry has discovered the Negro consumer as an economic power.

Complex transitional patterns may be discerned in this regard. The spatial concentration of Negroes will operate over decades as a factor of separation. The prosperous Negroes in their newly-built suburbias, who have finally succeeded in rising within their own middle class, will show an even greater *vis inertiae* than the Negroes in the slums. Purely Negro communities, like Mound Bayou in Mississippi, founded without any assistance from whites, are esteemed by Negroes, including those who prefer to seek social advancement in the cities dominated by whites, as symbols and proofs of the abilities of their race.

Racial pride is not confined to the whites. For Negroes, it finds justification in the success of a few extraordinarily talented individuals who have won fame and fortune in the white world as artists, writers or scholars. On the other hand, racial pride excludes the outside world.

Some Negroes complain that the lifting of racial segregation would lead to the movement of the all too few trained colored individuals from colored business to "integrated" federal agencies or enterprises in the North. And it is, of course, quite true that, economically speaking, the "marginal utility" of Negro businesses is far greater than it could be in a free, integrated, competitive market, and that they therefore stand to lose in the future.

Conflicts emerge out of these contradictions. A closed Negro society at the lowest rungs of the social ladder is slowly being replaced by a more mobile, economically differentiated society, in which hitherto unknown class tensions are developing among Negroes themselves. A Negro upper class exists, with more sophisticated demands. In a survey entitled *Black Bourgeoisie,* Franklin Frazier, sociology professor at the Negro university in Washington, describes this class structure, with merciless criticism, as a farce and an aping of the white upper class.

Although living in the cities, in the southern states, does not yet make Negroes free, yet the only way to advancement, at least for the next generation, leads through the cities. In 1900, ninety per cent of all Negroes lived in the South, two-thirds of them in the rural plantation areas. Today one-third of all Negroes—about six million—still live on the land in the South, one-third in the southern cities and one-third in the northern states (mainly in the cities). The racial problem has therefore become essentially an urban problem. The astonishingly rapid industrialization of the South, initiated by the establishment of munitions works there during the Second World War, attracted millions of Negroes to the cities, although fewer than whites, for the mechanization of agriculture has squeezed out the poor whites just as it has the poor Negroes. The Negroes who have moved into the cities from the rural areas are completely unequipped to meet the difficult requirements of a technological civilization; but the same does not necessarily apply to their children. The colored society which has developed in the southern cities, partly strictly segregated, partly linked with the white society by the "creeping integration" of economic working procedures, can be described somewhat as follows:

The approximately 100,000 professionals and others who constitute the prosperous middle class in the South—some 1.6 per cent of the urban Negro population—have all reached their high positions exclusively through their work in Negro communities. They include doctors, teachers, professors, ministers, journalists, publishers, real estate dealers, insurance agents, store-keepers, and restaurant owners. Wherever opportunities for advancement involve a measure of racial integration, they are either nil or infinitesimal. Thus, for instance, in the whole of the South there are barely five hundred Negro engineers as against 100,00 white ones. That explains why the pyramid of the well-paid trades and professions does not broaden smoothly toward the base. In the industrial field, Negroes are excluded not only from executive posts but also, for the most part, from skilled or supervisory jobs. They are to be found again, in large numbers, only at the lowest levels of unskilled or unpleasant work. For industry is in white hands, and white unions see to it that Negro workers do not so easily reach the assembly line. The relationship between Negro and union leaders is equivocal. In matters of social ethics they are on the same side, but the Negro elite is increasingly critical of the AFL-CIO, because union practice all too rarely corresponds to its ethical code in matters of equal rights for Negroes within the organized labor force.

Except in the construction and automobile industries, Negroes are confined to the lowest forms of employment. They are employed as truck-drivers, porters, janitors, and other jobs which never lead to skilled work or higher wages. Nevertheless, even the lowest wages in the cities are higher than the Negroes can make in the rural South, where they still live in rush-roofed, wooden huts, protected by stilts against the constantly encroaching swamps, just like the lake dwellings of prehistory. The Negro leaders hope that more and more factories will employ colored workers in higher posts, too. The southern branches of northern firms have already made a start in this direction, often in the face of a powerful boycott of their goods by the White Citizens' Councils, and federal government services do so as a matter of principle. A city in a particularly race-conscious region of Alabama, for instance, has two hundred colored postal officials and letter-carriers. So far only a very small minority of Negro workers has benefited from this policy. But—again to quote the sociology professor of the Negro university of Atlanta—hope of advancement is the drive that sustains all American minorities, regardless of color. Hope for tomorrow is a typically American trait.

This hope has drawn millions of Negroes to the North—anywhere, that is, but the South—where they live in concentrations which have become politically influential. Here they possess one power: the ballot. The mobile city life, where there is no legal discrimination, makes it easier for the Negro to break out of the prison of his skin. But here, too, there are social barriers, no less effective by remaining for the most part invisible. The panic which tends to grip a middle-class suburb when a Negro family succeeds in penetrating it has become a favorite theme of the novelist. But there are also examples of the contrary. Many years ago, a Negro family bought one of the beautiful old houses near the University of Chicago, in a select academic community. Some of the white families at once sold their houses, but the rest decided together to maintain the high standard of their neighborhood and gained the willing cooperation of the Negro family. The area retained its distinguished character.

It is one of the greatest American paradoxes that the Federal Government spends enormous sums every year to protect the "developing areas" throughout the world from Communist contagion by raising their living standards, while in the South, millions of American citizens find their way to advancement barred. And there may be some truth in the complaint of Negro intellectuals that the general political climate of moderation, in the fifties, made it possible for the extremists in the South to turn back the clock without arousing any passionate protest throughout the country. But what is chiefly true is that it is only a few in the deep South —that enchanting region of the United States—who set the shrill tone in this controversy of worldwide significance. Here, too, the free American society seeks to find ways and means, if only sporadic, and very slow, of dealing with its opponents.

One example of this process was the successful Negro student movement of non-violent "sit-in" protests. Another was the Freedom Riders. As the records of the Southern Regional Council show, at least ninety-five communities, located in ten southern states, had desegregated their lunch counters by 1962, as a result of the sit-in demonstrations. Segregation in travel facilities is expected to disappear soon. The Supreme Court ruled at the beginning of 1962: "We have settled beyond question that no state may require racial segregation of interstate or intrastate transportation facilities." The stepped-up tempo would hardly be conceivable if the organized Negro movement was not more strongly conscious than ever before of the support of the Federal Government. When the first serious racial conflict under the Kennedy Administration arose, in Alabama in May, 1961, the Attorney-General firmly applied the legal and coercive measures available to the Federal Government to protect the colored (and some white) participants in a non-violent demonstration against racial inequality, from the white mob. But he also used his influence to persuade the Negro elite to modify their Gandhi-like civil disobedience, on the grounds that militancy, even non-violent, breeds counterpressures and, therefore, increased racial antagonisms.

It is hardly surprising that, in spite of everything, the pace of integration in the South is not rapid enough for the Negro leaders. The Rev. Martin Luther King, Jr., writes that the Negroes' "sense of inadequacy is heightened when they look at Africa and Asia and see with envy the bursting of age-old bonds in societies still partially at a tribal level, but ablaze with modern vitality and creativity. An Alliance for Progress for South America, to cost $20 billion, is forward-looking and necessary. An Alliance for Progress for the turbulent South is equally necessary . . ." Pressure is now being put on the South from a long way off.

But Dr. King, if he is naturally impatient, attests that President Kennedy "has begun 1962 with a show of renewed aggressiveness; one can only hope that it will be sustained."

That the somber passions aroused in white and colored alike by the whole question of skin color should have fascinated novelists is hardly surprising. What is more surprising is the influence which literature has had on the realities of the race problem. *Uncle Tom's Cabin* has been called the most influential novel ever written. Lincoln is supposed to have described the author, Harriet Beecher Stowe, when she was presented to him, as "the little lady who wrote the book that made this great war." "The little lady," a Calvinist, later maintained that God was the real author. If that was the case, then the effect He gave the book was different from the one she had planned. Instead of healing the rift between South and North, as Mrs. Stowe had hoped, her story of the suffering of plantation Negroes, written in a sentimental vein and without real knowledge of the facts, became an explosive that kindled the crusading mood in the North and drove the South into still greater hatred of the Yankees. Perhaps even worse—for the Civil War was inevitable, even without Harriet Beecher Stowe—this book which every child reads has to this day left a series of distorted stereotypes in the American subconscious, and to that extent slows down the rational removal of the legacy of slavery.

A little over a hundred years after the publication of *Uncle Tom's Cabin* (1852), J. C. Furnas, in *Goodbye to Uncle Tom,* debunked the Harriet Beecher Stowe legend by revealing the factual misjudgments and the unreliability of the well-intentioned work. One of the most disastrous effects of the maudlin portrait of the Negro in *Uncle Tom's Cabin* was that it contributed to the precipitate reforms launched by the victorious North, which in their turn resulted in an even more severe setback for the colored race, from which it has not yet recovered. A modern historian writes: "No small part of the incredible optimism with which the North later approached the task of converting slaves into voters, self-dependent citizens and legislators, thinking it could be done overnight, is chargeable to the impression diffused by Mrs. Stowe."

That *Uncle Tom's Cabin* performed a treacherous service to the colored race comes out most clearly in the fact that the name, which should have enjoyed hero-worship among Negroes, has become for them a term of abuse. Furnas reports what a Negro told him: the epithet "Uncle Tom" in its earliest connotation meant "a boot-licking, servile type of Negro in his relationship with the whites." Now, he goes on, "it may mean a weakling or a coward, a traitor, a wily manipulator, one who engineers a race sell-out."

The overlapping of two irrationalities, race and sex, seems always to have held particular fascination for novelists, even if in their presentations, these demons usually act upon each other in self-destructive fashion. The reality of the sexual element in the old plantation civilization of the South, however, was of an animal simplicity, even if not altogether undemonic. As a result of his condition, the Negro slave tended inevitably to promiscuity; living as he did scarcely above the animal level, sexual relations were virtually his only recreation. Moreover, since the plantation master was very interested in the augmentation of his work force, he encouraged sexual activity among his slaves, whether monogamous or not, and also cared for the offspring. But we also know from many contemporary writings that the master, his adolescent sons and the white overseers made a habit of taking part in this increase; the countless mulatto children (the very light among them had a chance to sneak their way into the white community) were the visible proof. The whites had their Negro concubines. Many plantation masters liked to be served at table by their own children. Sometimes, even, a master would sell his half-caste children on the slave market.

The white ladies did their best to ignore the phenomenon. Mary Chestnut wrote about the plantations in South Carolina: "Like the patriarchs of old, our men live all in one house with their wives and their concubines, and the mulattoes one sees in every family party resemble the white children." Even Jefferson had colored mistresses and children from them; it is said that he acquiesced when his light-skinned offspring fled to freedom.

This whole domain, as sultry as the air of the South, has of course tempted literary minds. Eugene O'Neill in *All God's Chillun Got Wings* presents a black-white *danse macabre* in a Strindberg mood: a young Negro and a fallen white girl drive themselves in their marriage to the point of madness and destruction. Erskine Caldwell describes whites who through frequent relations with Negro women have lost the power to love a white woman. In his *Estherville,* two mulatto sisters fall into a kind of involuntary prostitution through the lust they inspire in white men and women. W. J. Cash, in his important analysis, *The Mind of the South,* maintains that the lust of the whites was provoked by the "natural" way Negro girls gave themselves, of which white women were incapable. However that may be, literature, spearheaded by the greatest novelist of the South, Faulkner, has always portrayed the black-white sexual pattern in macabre tones.

O'Neill's play, *Emperor Jones,* reaches an artistic translucency which illumines the tragic theme. Following Jung's doctrine of the collective subconscious, O'Neill has the images of the Negro destiny pass through a modern Negro soul whose deepest levels are aroused under the influence of fear while an African drum sounds with muffled and regular beat: from the present, through slavery times in the southern American states, back to the human sacrifices in the African jungle—where it all began.

7.

The Self-conscious Eros

THE extent of analysis of sex mores in the United States is overwhelming. Something must surely be amiss if this most private of domains invites so much public self-criticism.

We asked the bookseller—realizing suddenly the irony of the situation and therefore hesitating a trifle—whether he had a copy of *The Decline of the American Male*. He had, and sold it to us with a smile. The jacket, by Robert Osborne, depicts a flesh-colored female figure dangling a grey manikin on a string, like a puppet, while the manikin writes out a check. It did not seem to worry the bookseller that the authors—three courageous *Look* editors—were making him earn his living on his own decline. Perhaps it is not a decline at all, but a transition? Certainly, few American males would dispute that something very radical has been taking place in the relationship between the sexes since around the Second World War, and that this something has not made their position stronger. Yet there is no trace of any male protest against this state of affairs.

The roots of this "sex revolution" go deeper than the Second World War. The male has forfeited much of his authority, but the female, in assuming it, has also assumed new burdens. Perhaps the immediate consequence of this revolution is not so much the decline of the male as an unspoken state of conflict between the sexes. Nowhere but in America could a collection of sketches like James Thurber's have appeared, graphically describing the "war between men and women," with the most caustic thrusts aimed at women. Thurber is among those who hold that America is actually a matriarchy, that women hold the reins, and not just since the war. In his drawings, the woman sometimes capitulates to the man, but she always has a stick or a rock behind her back. The war, as far as she is concerned, goes on . . .

Philip Wylie, in his avidly read *Generation of Vipers,* created the concept of "momism," according to which the American matriarchy begins with the domination of the boy by his mother. The boy may rebel, but in so doing he only entangles himself more irrevocably in her apron strings, subsequently transferring this relationship to his wife. Wylie expresses the hostility of the male to the opposite sex. Yet woman is adulated in American life in a manner more frankly erotic than in any other civilization at any time. This hostility and this adulation belong, so it seems, to the basic ingredients of love.

Why, ask the analysts of love, do women dominate the American male? They, too, begin with "momism." The principal instrument of education is no longer the punitive power of the father but the love of the mother, doled out according to the boy's behavior. Then comes school, where most of the teachers are women; the classroom is already a competing ground with girls. In high school and college, the sexual freedom which youth has been taking for barely more than a decade has led to a female advantage which later reaches into marriage. The late Dr. Kinsey, with his human zoology, made it his business to shed the cold light of scientific investigation on what is essentially a pagan revolution in sexual behavior.

At fourteen or fifteen, teenage eroticism comes into play, tolerated by society and parents, half encouraged and half feared. The motives prompting such encouragement are, in a unique way, American. Parents want to prove themselves to be good Americans through their children. The love which their youngsters arouse, they identify with success—the success of social adjustment. Consequently, they urge their children to assert themselves in competition with their contemporaries. And in this regard, there is no more important criterion than to be "popular"—to have a lot of dates, to be erotically courted or successful. A youngster who stays home too many evenings a week (who in Europe would be regarded simply as self-willed or in need of privacy) testifies to the failure of his parents; he may even be suspected of being schizophrenic. The early anticipation of adult sexual behavior becomes a condition of social assertiveness or at least of social conformity.

Margaret Mead, who has investigated teenagers as much as she has investigated Samoan natives, commented on this very revealing attitude: "Children," she wrote, "are drawn into the dating game not by their bodies, but by their assertiveness, their desire to achieve, to succeed, to be popular. Yet the game is cast in highly sexual terms. Viewed from the standpoint of another culture, or even from a recent visit to one's own unconscious, this all gives a picture of a people, especially a youth group, who are tremendously preoccupied with sex, whose only interest in life is love, and whose definition of love is purely physical. Yet this seems to me to be an enormous misstatement. Rather, this continuous emphasis on the sexually relevant physical appearance is an outcome of using a heterosexual game as the prototype for success and popularity in adolescence."

This view is borne out by the practice, carried sometimes to the point of degeneracy, of female teenagers who are in the habit of greeting their heroes, the young crooners—the one best known being Elvis Presley, of the writhing hips and thighs—with a shrill lascivious yell that seems to issue from a single throat. The picture of young and well-dressed girls comporting themselves in this fashion is enough to send cold shivers down an adult's spine. Significantly, however, it has been observed that only the girls in the rows lit up by the stage lights break out in this yell; that is, only those who can be seen by the others. Moreover, they are looking not so much at the singer as at the other members of their own group. The uproar, therefore, is not simply an expression of collective lust directed towards the male hero on the stage, but even more an expression of teenage "belonging"—belonging to that new, strange world which has become a pseudo-adult world, separated from the real adult world by the lost understanding between the generations, not yet tested by the teenagers' own adulthood.

The special world of the eighteen million teenagers who are growing up in the United States, living only physically in their families, has become a subject of investigation in much the same way as other exotic cultures. Thomas B. Morgan has been, perhaps, one of the most ruthless in pulling aside the veil of sentiment which seeks to hide the dominant fact of the new kind of estrangement between adults and children. The heads and hearts of the teenagers, he writes, are usually in their own teen-land. They are fully conscious teenagers, as their parents never were. They feel themselves to be an independent race, a minority in a strange land. That is why, Morgan concludes, they cling with savage pride to a private variety of mores as mysterious to those on the outside as they are bewildering.

Can it be that the extraordinary success of *Lolita,* the diabolical story of a teenage "nymphet," by Vladimir Nabokov, conveys the melancholy message that the gulf between the two worlds can now be bridged only by desperate perversion? *Lolita* is about a shrewd, elegant European of uncertain Danubian extraction, in his forties, who loves a twelve-year-old girl in America and, legally speaking, rapes her. (But it turns out that the sexual act was, anyway, no novelty to her.) He lives with her for two years, travels with her, in constant flight from the eyes of society, all over the United States, finally loses her, shoots his rival and dies in prison of a heart attack. But before he dies he writes his memoirs—the novel. All this, however grotesque it may sound, is told with sardonic wit, with a kind of superior detachment on the part of the principal character (Humbert Humbert, a name which "expresses the nastiness best"). Nabokov writes so well that one of the best-known American literary critics, Lionel Trilling, astonished at his own reaction, writes: "we find ourselves the more shocked when we realize that, in the course of reading the novel, we have come virtually to condone the violation it presents."

Nabokov calls his schoolgirl Undine—a "nymphet." "Nymphets," are beings whom Humbert Humbert exactly defines: "Between the age limits of nine and fourteen there occur maidens who, to certain bewitched travellers, twice or many times older than they, reveal their true nature which is not human but nymphic (that is, demonic); and these chosen creatures I propose to designate as 'nymphets.'" Lolita, with her solid bourgeois name—Dolores Haze—is such a nymphet. She is loved hopelessly and self-destructively by the perverse "H.H." (as he calls himself in his prison memoirs). *Lolita,* writes Nabokov, who published his first novels in Russian as far back as 1924, has "no moral in tow." But neither does he reveal the idea which inspired this novel, which upsets the last social taboo still valid in the sphere of sex—the sexual inviolability of girls who are still children. Nabokov implies that he sets no great store by ideas. He expresses himself rather disparagingly about Gorki and Thomas Mann. Only Proust seems to enjoy his esteem. Lionel Trilling offers an interpretation of *Lolita* which is more convincing than anything else that has been said about the shocking book, and that is not little. In our sober, conformist society, he maintains, passionate love, or passion, suffered by the lover as something pathological, the kind of love known to European literature since the age of the minstrels, is no longer possible.

It is incompatible with the contemporary—and particularly the American—ideal of love as a tolerant, firm, happy, healthy marriage. Nabokov's novel would then signify that absolute love today can exist only in the form of what for a bourgeois society is a desperate perversion. "*Lolita,*" Trilling writes, "is about love. Almost every page sets forth some explicit erotic emotion or some overt erotic action, and still it is not about sex. It is about love."

Youth's accession to independence cannot be understood without reference to the role of psychology. Just as the Soviet Russian society was the first revolutionary offspring of a scientific system—Marxism—so American society is the first in history where psychoanalysis has become a socially constitutive force. The collapse of parental authority—the reverse side of teenage emancipation—is a direct consequence of the ideas received at second- or third-hand about the harm that "forcible" education can inflict on a child's soul in the form of complexes, repressions and inhibitions. Such psychiatric reasonings have bewildered parents and replaced character-forming by a tolerant form of education that is more permissive than restrictive, more persuasive than authoritarian. The advances of modern medicine in the last ten years have largely removed the fear of contagious disease; that fear has been replaced by fears concerning the mental health of children. Out of this pedagogical over-rationalization there has issued the breed which dismays its parents from the age of twelve by its attacks of mass hysteria in theatres. After this phase, at about the age of fifteen, there begins a no less strange individual existence, rendered mobile by the car, governed by an erotic code which even organized religious bodies take as a fact. For $.25 one can buy a YMCA booklet entitled "Facts of Life and Love for Teenagers" which lays down the rules of the game and lists their transgressions in the early relations between the sexes.

At an age when formerly the sexes shunned each other or observed each other with timidity and reserve, there begins the eroticism of touch known as necking and petting, with its own rules. Theoretically this goes no farther than a preliminary game, with fleeting touches, and the young partners are largely interchangeable. Dating was at first a form of authorized youthful experimentation, involving frequent and deliberate changes of principals. This promiscuity without responsibility corresponded more to the biological interests of the male, though what was new in it was the freedom given to young girls by their parents, this being a further step in the emancipation of woman. The transformation which early teenage eroticism has undergone in the last ten years is regarded by the scientific experts in the field—psychologists, sociologists and doctors—as further evidence of the dominance of the female. A kind of monogamy has established itself even prior to marriage, the pattern of "going steady," which has replaced the rapid interchangeability of dating. Now the very young, teenagers still of school age, go "steady"; they appear as miniature married couples *vis-à-vis* their contemporaries, who also pair off in miniature married couples. Thus, the longing for emotional security even at the adolescent stage corresponds to the adult striving for complete social integration.

The longing for emotional security may be equally strong on both sides, but the male partner sacrifices his inherent tendency to make his first erotic experiments at his pleasure, since he has to start off right away with firm loyalties. That is undoubtedly a triumph for the female, to whom biology now deals the stronger hand. For in "going steady" the girl inevitably makes the decisions as to how far the couple should go in their petting practices. The frequent changes involved in dating, apparently more amoral, in fact, of course, drew the limits more closely. The constant association of a "steady" couple, on the other hand, tends just as naturally to extend the limits of the teenager relationship. The rising number of illegitimate births and absurdly young forced marriages shows that the limits have often been transgressed altogether. The rule is that the girl applies the brakes; and the power which she thereby acquires is retained in marriage, whether the "steady" youth partner becomes the husband, or another.

This has given rise to what Maxine Davis calls, in a book of the same name, the "sexual responsibility of women." Not only, so the argument runs, has the woman the same right to sexual satisfaction as the man—a right contended for repeatedly in the battle against the Puritan-*cum*-Victorian heritage—but she must also take some responsibilities from him in the marriage act. The female reader is told that she is co-responsible for the happy, uninhibited fulfillment of love in marriage, and she is given very detailed instructions. Basically this is only the extension of the responsibility of the girl in teenage eroticism, as described by Margaret Mead: "The controls of this dangerous game that is so like a ski-slide, yet which must never be treated as a ski-slide, are placed in the hands of the girl . . . From this game, played over and over again, sometimes for ten years or so before marriage, arises the later picture of married life in America, in which it is the wife who sets the pattern of sex relations."

We find in all this an inordinate stress on the rational, a passion for the rational analysis of erotic processes, a rationalization of sex which mechanically isolates the sexual from other intimate spheres of life instead of leaving it its spontaneity, which is fed by other sources than merely its own. That is perhaps the deepest reason why the problem of love is so incessantly debated among Americans. The rational approach is characteristically linked with the enhanced position of the woman. The consensus of the marriage counselors —mostly psychiatrically trained and scattered in thousands across the country—is that the most urgent duty of the male,

contrary to age-old practice, is to consider the sexual satisfaction of the female. Hence, Maxine Davis tells her women
readers: "The wife must make her husband realize, as he
gladly will, how important it is that she be satisfied. She must
be wholly satisfied; she cannot accept compromises." American men have evidently learned this precept, for, as Professor
McHugh of Duke University writes, "most American men
blame themselves if their wives fail to achieve complete
marital happiness." Another expert, a psychoanalyst, dis-
penses cold comfort to American men, saying that they might
as well reach for the moon as try to fulfill all these "obli-
gations." But it seems that they want to reach for the moon.
And they are helped in this endeavor, as are their wives, by
the sex manuals.

The trend towards rationalization, and also its dangers, become evident in the wide dissemination of these scientific
text books on sex, apparently already a kind of compulsory
reading for young couples. The basic, anti-Victorian contention of these manuals is that the woman, like the man, is
entitled to the physical fulfillment of love, and that the man
must see to it that both partners reach orgasm simultaneously.
Precise instructions are given to this end. From the point of
view of the sex manuals, which are read by millions and
whose teachings are also reflected in the popular magazines,
the criterion of a good or bad marriage is reduced to the
ability to achieve simultaneous orgasm; they offer the technique, and assume that after that everything else will take
care of itself.

In reality, this philosophy can just as well—or better—be
reversed, and it can be contended that the physical pleasure
curves, which the sexual manuals so touchingly show on
graphs, will meet of themselves if the rest is taken care of.
The "rest" may be defined as the totality of psychic and
emotional experience from which the prevailing theory seeks
to separate the act of love as such, making that act central to

the whole. Serious marriage counselors have meanwhile begun to warn unhappy couples not to overestimate the purely physical.

What they are saying has nothing to do with asceticism, which would find little enough response in a society which alternates between Puritanism and hedonism; their warning is of a different sort. Couples whose physical satisfaction leaves something to be desired are deceived into regarding this fact as indicative of some fault in their marriage. Instead of being patient, they become panicky; their whole marriage seems to them to have failed, and mechanically learned techniques easily break down. Thus the manuals, which are merely symptomatic of the general tendency toward rationalization, achieve a result exactly contrary to the one intended: they do not heal marriages but generate uncertainty. The equations: sexual attraction equals love, and love equals marriage, result in the vicious circle which keeps the divorce rate so high. The marriage based on excessive physical expectations is broken up, but it is immediately renewed with a different cast, precisely because—at least after the teenage stage—extra-marital sexual relations are socially taboo, even if they occur in fact. So we get the paradox that the frequent divorces reflect respect for the institution of marriage rather than the contrary.

One cannot help thinking that the emphasis on a rational approach to love—connected, as we shall see, with an irrational antipole—reflects a degree of mechanization of American civilization. Of course, the belief in boundless possibilities also enters into it. But the urge to find rational formulae to keep a couple together has still another cause, arising out of the character of this society. On this point, the psychologists of marriage counseling have most experience. One marriage counseling bureau, in Philadelphia, has, for nearly thirty years, been studying causes of the high divorce rate in the light of those cases in which assistance is sought (mostly husband and wife seek assistance together, though they are often interrogated separately). Every single day, over one thousand divorces are granted in the United States, twice the rate even of Sweden, four times that of England.

Behind the high divorce rate, according to the Philadelphia psychologists, is the circumstance that the great American melting pot does not fuse and unify as fast as one would like to think. The American experiment in living is conducted jointly, and at the same time competitively, by countless ethnic, racial and religious groups with their varied traditions, customs, beliefs, and instinctive reactions in the sphere of personal life (from the attitude towards the mother-in-law to erotic practices). The extraordinary mobility of the social order, in respect both to class and to geography, throws the members of all these groups on the marriage market, whether in college, university, place of work, the big city, or in the course of the incessant migrations across the continent. On this market, too, the theory of free supply and demand prevails. "We are all Americans," so the slogan runs, and again: "Marry if you love each other." This, of course, is part of basic Americanism, and most parents assuredly bring their children up to believe in it, at the same time hoping, in their heart of hearts, that the choice will be of a different kind. For, as we have said, the melting pot does not turn all those who enter it into synthetic Americans. Indeed, the contrary seems to be the case. The conservatism of human nature persists, and members of ethnic and religious groups still tend to marry within their own groups rather than outside them.

But, of course, a great and growing number do marry on the principle that the melting pot really eliminates differences. And they constitute the raw material of the specifically American divorce problem. The Philadelphia marriage counseling bureau reports on the dissensions arising in marriages between Russians, Poles, Irish, Italians, English, Spanish or Germans; or again—and here ethnic strains and religious ties overlap—in unions between Orthodox Jews and liberal Catholics, Quakers and Eastern European Jews, conservative Presbyterians and freethinkers; or, finally, when the daughter of a wealthy New England patrician marries the son of poor immigrants who can hardly speak English (not a common occurrence). More often than not, the marriage is entered into without lengthy family consultations. Then comes the acid test of the couple's relations with each other's families. At this point unexpected loyalties awaken, the crisis sets in and the couple turn to professional advisers for assistance. (But these advisers, too, with their conceptual world saturated with psychoanalysis, offer no panacea; they fail as often as they succeed in building a bridge between the spouses by pointing out the difficulties arising in marriage between members of different groups—that is, if they are not mere quacks dispensing patent medicines for the psyche.)

In any event, the "melting pot" situation, where ethnically mixed marriages are the rule and not the exception, inevitably encourages rational thought on the subject of sex. Only a communicable rationality—be it the mechanical teachings of the manuals or a tolerant understanding in regard to the irrational barriers of tradition—can ever hope to dissolve the conflicts generated in a marriage by home and church, by race and respectable prejudice.

The "war between men and women," we are told, is in full swing in America, and the men are frankly inclined to feel they are on the receiving end. But the woman too, as the evidence shows, has her burden to carry in a sociological transformation which is really less a decline of one side in the sexual relationship than a transition to a new form of this relationship. But this form is in many respects altogether novel. It has arisen because the hierarchical structure of the family has disintegrated to a degree as yet hardly to be imagined in Europe. The "democratic process," so lauded in the sphere of political education, has taken possession of

this most intimate unit of society. Husband, wife and child
are all, in some way, equal. Under the Puritan dispensation
they were still patriarchically ordered—the position of the
father being rooted in the Bible—whereas today they are in
the process of becoming a team. If the dethroned—but not
really rebellious—males call this new state of affairs a matriarchy, they can justify this description, at most, by pointing
out that women's emancipation was the catalyst in this development. But it seems that this emancipation has reached
its saturation point.

Women's emancipation took place later in the United States
than in the Old World. But, like the American industrial
revolution, the erotic revolution in America outpaced everything of the same order in Europe. Even at the point of
departure, women were at an advantage in America. They
had a scarcity value which they never enjoyed in Europe.
This explains the indissoluble association of a romantic concept of love with the institution of marriage which has become the obvious, yet exceedingly fragile, frame into which
love in America must ever be forced. What we know today
as the United States began without women; the first British
colony, Jamestown, consisted solely of men—little more than
one hundred. Apart from a few possible contacts with Indian
women, love, for the first settlers at least, could not have been
a heterosexual affair. When, shortly after, women were "im-
ported" from England, they had the privilege of choosing
their partners among the men, despite the obvious purpose—
childbearing in the New World—they had come to serve.
This has remained a characteristically American situation even
though America as a whole now has an excess of women.
In eight western states there are even today more men than
women, and any girl going from the East Coast to one of
these states can enjoy the scarcity value of women of the
pioneering days, and take advantage of it in choosing a husband.

Because of the original scarcity value of women, "romantic love" became the powerful and undisputed norm for young Americans of both sexes, and "romantic love" culminating in marriage became the natural pattern of sex relations. "True love," all evidence to the contrary notwithstanding, has been regarded ever since, both as spontaneously generated (instead of being prepared by family arrangement) and permanent. Young girls never had to regard themselves as adjuncts to a dowry, since that social practice did not exist; this was no bad starting point for the later emancipation of women, however extensive the authority of the *paterfamilias* in the early Puritan regime of the New England settlers.

The influence of Puritanism on American values cannot, of course, be overstimated, even if it is more honored in the breach than in the observance. Nevertheless, it would be wrong to ascribe to the New England Puritans of the seven- teenth and eighteenth centuries a fanatical hostility to every- thing sexual. Unlike Catholicism, Puritanism never upheld the ideal of virginity or of priestly continence. For Puritans, marriage was a civil contract, which is why they countenanced divorce. Their ministers married and eagerly obeyed the Biblical prescription to be fruitful and multiply, evidently unburdened by any sense of sin. Marriages in the Puritan colonies took place so unbelievably early—the girls often at fourteen or fifteen, the men under twenty—that there could be no problem at all of premarital relations. Strict Puritans re- fused sexual pleasure on Sundays; since this was regarded as a restriction, one may draw conclusions as to the rest of the week. The determining factor was not asceticism but morality: only procreation justifies sexuality. Historians of civilization believe that only when Puritanism was allied with late nineteenth-century Victorianism was that prudish fusti- ness developed which is now meant by "puritanical."

On the other hand, the role of Puritanism is unmistakable in the way love is monopolized by marriage. Romantic love—

regarded as the most genuine type of love—should not be hidden from society; but it may be acknowledged before the world only in the form of marriage. Hence, the frequency of remarriage among divorced persons. The trinity of romantic love, marriage monopoly and Puritan work ethos, incidentally, is not best suited to develop the faculty of charming frivolity. That is why European descriptions of America have always denied its people any talent for love, and legends have developed on the subject—for instance, the legend of the native frigidity of the American woman.

The matriarchal features of contemporary American society make one forget that here, too, woman had to fight for her rights for a whole century. Her present position of equality can be regarded as one of the most successful revolutions in world history—perhaps even too successful, as many women may secretly think. For the high price which American woman has had to pay for her ascent is that she may no longer be weak. She has shed this attribute of Eve, and, logically, the upper-class concept of a lady has finally had to be sacrificed too. She could not well retain the weapon of weakness and at the same time accumulate so much political, economic and erotic power as she has accumulated in the space of a few generations.

If it is sometimes said that the American woman is not only the wealthiest, physically healthiest, best dressed and most independent woman in the world, but also the most unhappy, this certainly has some connection with the surrender of the weapon of weakness. This surrender is paid for in the coin of neuroses. But this too may be only a transition to a new equilibrium which the victorious woman is striving to achieve. It all began around 1848, with the suffragette movement which, as in England, was contemptuously rebuffed by the male world, which identified feminism with atheism and communism. If the present state of affairs is ~ompared with the first beginnings of emancipation, one can hardly help sympathizing with the men who wanted to suppress the whole movement. The power situation has been so radically changed that the man is now being required to make it his first concern to ensure the sexual satisfaction of the woman.

Sociologists distinguish four separate revolutions leading to the present position of women. The same phases exist in Europe too, but in all of them the American woman has by far overshot the European mark.

The first was the revolution resulting in votes for women —but not until 1920—and the right to equal education and access to leadership in politics and industry. Today women hold high government office, they are ambassadors, public prosecutors, bankers, general managers and, at least, vice-presidents of great firms. Woman's ascent in the modern professional and labor world is truly staggering. Generally speaking, the distinction between man and woman as far as economic efficiency is concerned has almost disappeared. It is only logical that in a recent discussion about the prospects of a woman becoming President of the United States, the only impediment suggested was that she could not very well fulfill the presidential role of commander in chief of the armed forces.

In 1920, there were eight million women working; in 1960, 22.7 million (as compared with 43.7 million men), and the Bureau of Census projects the figure of twenty-eight million for 1970. Statistics for 1960 show the total money income of working women to amount to $43.8 billion. Sixty per cent of all working women are married—a significant figure. Their average age is over forty. Today ninety per cent of all women—or virtually all women—have held jobs from time to time. It is estimated that a girl who has gone through high school—and that means virtually all girls—will spend an average of twenty-five years of her life at work. The American woman works not only between school or university and marriage, but increasingly returns to work after some fifteen years as a housewife and mother. It may be to buy herself a fur coat, to help finance the terribly expensive college education of her children, or simply to keep busy, but the most prevalent reason is that of economic necessity in a highly competitive society.

Women are presidents of banks, they sit on boards of directors, they serve in a managerial capacity in industry, and of course they are to be found in great numbers in the teaching, nursing and medical professions. Whole industries would have to shut down if the women employed in them suddenly decided to stop working; schools, hospitals, banks, telephone companies, insurance companies, government agencies and many light industries employ more women than men. One-third of all women are now permanently employed, but in the future, if the country is to maintain its standard of living and its rate of growth, the number of working women will have to increase—by about five million by 1965, so it has been calculated—and at all levels of the economic chain of command. They have become indispensable.

The second revolution was the sexual revolution in the narrower sense, the revolt against the dual "standard" in morals, which permitted to man what it forbade to woman. (But since in any case extra-marital relations were not of such frequent occurrence, the conquest in this domain was not so great.) The specific victory consists in the re-evaluation of the sexual claims of woman within the marriage, to which we have already referred.

Thirdly, there took place a revolution in manners; women were permitted to smoke in public, even in the street, to drink, to dress just as casually as the men, to bare their bodies in a most unpuritanical way, to drive cars and pilot planes.

The fourth revolution took place in the home (particularly in the kitchen); it consisted in the release of woman from the creaturely, never-ending burdens of the household through the mechanization of household appliances and the availability of built-in labor services in the form of frozen and canned foods. This, in turn, hastened the economic revolution.

The economic power of women is not confined to their role as workers; indirectly it is much greater. When the term "economic matriarchy" is used, it is this indirect power that is envisaged. According to John Karol, a vice-president of CBS radio and television—and he should know, since his transmissions are financed by commercials—women are the real queens of economic life and the goddesses of the advertising business. As a consumer, as the mistress of the family household, the woman disposes of the greatest part of the purchasing power. According to one sociologist, women control up to seventy per cent of the American national wealth and sixty per cent of savings. They constitute up to seventy per cent of the beneficiaries of life insurance policies, they represent more than half the stockholders of big firms, and they own nearly half of all houses in the country.

The most disconcerting of these figures is that relating to the proportion of stockholders; even some of the giant concerns, such as General Electric, Du Pont, United States Steel, belong—from the point of view of stocks—to women. Most of the women, of course, have acquired stocks, bonds and real estate as the widows and heiresses of their overworked husbands. (The American woman has become a tough species; her average life span exceeds that of the American man by six years—73 to 67.) There remains the masculine revenge, that as managers, bankers, lawyers and executors, men retain the managerial control of the wealth whose ownership they have forfeited.

Despite all these newly won powers, or perhaps precisely because of them, the indications are that the forty-five million married women in the United States are not really able to enjoy their ascendancy. Neuroses, as reported by doctors, the frightening number of abortions (even among married women, as the third Kinsey report showed), divorces, increasing alcoholism (especially in suburbia, those idyllic settlements surrounding the cities, where other stimulants are absent), have raised the question of why, at the height of her triumph, the American woman is not happier. What appears as the "decline of the American male" seems to be for her, too, no untrammeled pleasure.

The anti-feminists have their answer ready: the man-like woman, this new Amazon of a technological civilization, this he-woman (the counterpart of the she-man) has overreached herself. She has become delirious in her power. The reality must be both less simple and less alarming. If only because American civilization is based emphatically on monogamy, the woman, however independent she may be, will in the first place seek the married status, that is, the man. She will also, supported by a sophisticated—and democratized—cosmetics and fashion industry, take trouble to look attractive, to be, if possible, slim, long-legged, provocative and paying tribute to the absurd bosom-fetishism of the film world. But that is not all.

This society, in which woman has succeeded in conquering such an outstanding position, nevertheless remains basically masculine, suffused with power impulses, with power conflicts of an almost violent nature. It is not easy for a woman who wishes to retain her independence to affirm herself in this society. What is hardest is to fulfill the incredible variety of functions incumbent upon her, without failing in the unavoidable, biological duty which the feminist movement underestimated, that of being simply a woman.

Modern American society offers the most extreme contrast to the old Chinese cultural pattern. Whereas in the latter, a woman was respected and influential the older she grew, in America the young glamour girl who kindles the romantic

ardor which leads irresistibly to marriage is the self-pre-
scribed ideal, after which there can be nothing but gradual
decline. Not to depart too sharply from this narrow beauty
cliché even as the years relentlessly take their toll, and at the
same time to play the many parts which emancipation have
brought her—that is an existence which truly deserves the
description which a social analyst has used as a chapter heading, "the ordeal of the American woman." According to this
scholar, the modern American woman "leads simultaneously
a multiplicity of lives, playing at once the role of sexual
partner, mother, home manager, hostess, nurse, shopper,
figure of glamour, supervisor of the children's schooling and
play and trips, culture audience and culture carrier, club-
woman, and often worker and careerist." Adlai Stevenson,
for his part, presents the position of the educated woman as
stripped of all romanticism since the dying out of the servant
class. In former times, he says, such women would talk art
and philosophy late into the night; now they are so tired
that their eyes close as soon as the dishes are put away. They
used to write poetry; now they write laundry lists.

The sociological background of love in America is full of
tensions unknown to more traditional civilizations. American
love, itself already full of tensions, is underpinned by these
sociological tensions.

The inhabitants of the United States, before the nineteen-
twenties an erotically boring, prudish, unimaginative people,
seem to have been swept by an anti-puritan reaction. This is
the impression which, reduced to the three-letter word SEX,
constantly confronts one. No single subject is more talked
about, written about, discussed, filmed, photographed, sung
about or studied. The whole teenage world too, deliberately
closed to adults, with its border cases of juvenile delinquency
and the group mystique of the gang, is naturally tied up with
the "sexual revolution" which has so alarmingly opened up

the premarital sphere. A young girl of purely middle-class background stated in a college discussion: "Sex is like raw meat. When you're hungry, you grab it." Pitirim Sorokin, the conservative Christian sociologist of Harvard University, wrote in his *The American Sex Revolution* (1956) that America was flooded with sexuality: "Whatever aspect of our culture is considered, each is packed with sex obsession . . . If we escape from being stirred by obscene literature, we may be aroused by the crooners, or by the new psychology and sociology, or by the teachings of the Freudianized pseudo-religions, or by radio-television entertainment. We are completely surrounded by the rising tide of sex which is flooding every compartment of our culture, every section of our social life. Unless we develop an inner immunity against these libidinal forces, we are bound to be conquered by the continuous army of omnipresent sex stimuli."

This "sexual hysteria," as others have called it, has provoked a dismal increase in the number of illegitimate births among girls of fifteen and under. Between 1949 and 1959, such births increased fourfold. In Washington, in thirteen schools, illegitimate births increased by one thousand per cent; in New York, in a single year, 1,250 unwedded mothers under fifteen were dismissed from school; in the port city of Baltimore, half of all illegitimate births were of teenage parents. In the whole of America, about forty per cent of all unmarried mothers were minors; of 183,000 illegitimate births in one year, minors accounted for 72,800. These numbers are less appalling if one remembers the size of the country. The class of female teenagers numbers some eight million; among them, therefore, much less than one per cent are unmarried mothers. Nevertheless, the existence of so many unwedded minor mothers is a social problem of the first order, which Americans are handling with characteristic kindness and helpfulness. Special birth clinics have been established, arrangements are made for supervised adoption (which does not, however, exclude a black market in babies), private sponsors assist the pregnant girls, who are thus enabled to bring their children into the world in protective anonymity.

The increase in teenage pregnancies is credited to the teenage practice of "going steady" as a form of premarital monogamy. But this practice is only a part of the general anti-puritanical, anti-Victorian reaction. On this point Dr. Goodrich C. Schauffler, the gynecologist, who has had many years' experience in the treatment of young patients, has said: ". . . youngsters, instead of being sheltered and disciplined as they once were, are now exposed to the seamy side of sex in its rawest forms before they have the faintest concept of its total meaning in life. We have only to look about us to realize that, as a nation, we are preoccupied—almost obsessed —with the superficial aspects of sex, with sex as a form of amusement. This is not true sex, with the corollaries of love, marriage and childbearing. It is an almost hysterical bandying about of sex symbols, coming close to fetish worship. (Consider the present over-emphasis of the breast, the stressing of erotic qualities in perfume.)"

An explanation suggests itself for this phenomenon which, to all appearances, permeates American civilization. It is this: the physical aspect of sex is isolated from the context of life as a whole. That is what makes it diabolical. It is taken too seriously, and again not seriously enough, because the faculty of being a channel of the spiritual is not granted it. The anti-puritan reaction has one thing in common with the puritanical view of sex—isolation. For Puritanism envisaged sex from the purely functional point of view of procreation; any other aspect of sex was sinful.

This isolation of the sexual—and this is, perhaps, its most serious consequence—seriously curbs spontaneity in lovemaking. With all the "sexual obsessions" which the social analysts deplore, there is no question of any great frivolity in American life. Openly to have a sweetheart or a mistress alongside his wife—such Latin pleasures are not easily forgiven an American, however wealthy. All the sexual stimuli with which—as Professor Sorokin laments—the modern news, advertising, and entertainment media saturate the American atmosphere, result for the individual American only in the monopolizing of love by marriage. And the Harvard scholar was quite wrong in predicting that the home would soon become "a mere overnight parking space mainly for sex relationship." On the contrary, in the last fifteen years the urge of both husband and wife to place the family in the center of their common life has been steadily growing. As a result, America has been rejuvenated; in 1960 there were already fifty million children under fourteen, so that the number of teenagers is expected to have increased by sixty-three per cent by 1970. They will have correspondingly greater opportunities to disconcert the adult world.

This is the circle: love is, in the first place, sexual attraction (otherwise there is doubt whether it is the "real thing," that is, the romantic "one and only" love); it must lead to marriage, for only in marriage can it find its socially sanctioned fulfillment, on which American perfectionism is based; expectations are pitched at the highest key; if they are not fulfilled, if love, as physical attraction, does not remain as intensive as it was on the first day, then nagging doubts set in and there begins what can be called the terror of happiness in American society.

It has been said that the Americans are the only people who have taken the romantic ideal of the minstrels and troubadours seriously. It has also been said that they are in love with love. It is certain, in any case, that as a people, as a society, they have moved farthest away from any utilitarian arrangements regarding love and marriage. In this respect—apart, perhaps, from the dynastic arrangements of the really wealthy families—this "capitalist" society is really not capitalist; it does not subordinate sentiment to the profit urge.

On the contrary, it would seem that this intensely technological civilization, that is, a civilization deliberately developed by man, wished to dedicate itself quite especially to the irrational, incalculable element of love. In the notion that love works on the principle of lightning, that suddenly, in a single instant of illumination, the encounter between two persons takes place which leads to marriage (after a previous history of search, of course, by means of "dating"); in this somewhat unwise and immature notion, American civilization renounces, for once at least, the idea of trying to plan, to foresee, to secure everything.

In this concept of love there is reflected the loneliness of the individual, which is such a very American phenomenon. The leap from loneliness to the opposite extreme of the unique romantic encounter, the correlation of two points in the social infinity, is psychologically valid. Other factors that enter into it are the mobility of society, the freedom with which classes and sexes mix, and also the rootlessness of a population constantly moving across this broad continent.

Of course, in all such observations on an intimate sphere of life one has to guard against over-generalizing. Love in conservative Boston is not the same as love in Los Angeles. Yet a common American trait is discernible: the tendency to make "happiness" the chief criterion. It is a tyrannical criterion, making excessive demands on human nature and human institutions. Because putting happiness to the test represents a constant challenge, the result is often exactly the reverse. The United States is the only nation on earth to have established the pursuit of happiness as a human right in a fundamental law of the Republic, the Declaration of Independence. Carried over from the reflective, leisurely spirit of the eighteenth century into the action world of the twentieth, the pursuit of this right can be a heavy burden.

A basic difference between the modern American and the

minstrel of the age of chivalry is that the minstrel's love lyrics were addressed extra-maritally, which is precisely not the case with the American. Romantic love, which the American immediately identifies with sexual attraction, must prove itself as the purveyor of happiness in marriage. If one is not happy in marriage, that is not only sad because happiness is absent, but it is even worse—in some way it is unconstitutional.

The evidence of a new, post-Christian hedonism in this prosperous society is unmistakable. Only a hedonistic consumer, after being proclaimed "sovereign" of the economic system, can play the part assigned to him. But when one sees what a burden the duty of happiness can be for many American couples, what a nagging process of self-examination it involves, one will agree with Max Lerner in dismissing the horrible suspicion that American marriage is "a mutual orgasm pact between two self-centered individuals." The constant concern of the spouses as to whether they are fulfilling each other's expectations is no small tribute to the civilization of happiness in which they live. Hence the reading of the manuals on sex technique; hence the paradoxical association of irrational romantic marriage (at least in theory) and rational analysis of the sexual relations between the spouses.

Behind the pursuit of happiness—which the Founding Fathers undoubtedly understood differently—a philosophy of life reminiscent of European attitudes after the turn of the century is gaining increasing currency. The obligation to live "intensively," not to let anything stand in the way of "experience," to "fulfill" oneself freely, to "express" oneself— these are phrases which constantly come up in the discussion of eroticism, and they were the language of expressionism, of youth movements, of anti-bourgeois sentiment before 1914. But because happiness is a constitutional right, the American striving for the uninhibited expression of personality is characteristically not anarchic; it is not aimed at disrupting existing institutions. Sex may still be confined to the twilight zone inherited from Puritanism, as the insincere moral code of Hollywood evidences, but where it is permitted to come into the open, in the premarital testing time and in marriage, there it is more unashamedly recognized as a purpose of existence than in any other western culture. If the marriage does not pass the test of happiness, equated with "sexual fulfillment," then this society is sufficiently experiment-happy to countenance a new endeavor through divorce and remarriage. The rising divorce rate, however, is not regarded as evidence of moral decline but as evidence of increasing receptiveness to the slogan: "Be happy, or you won't have lived!" This philosophy of happiness, once the sense of obligation it inculcates has been dulled, may well prove to be the solution to the "sexual revolution" which began more than four decades ago; it will make women gentler again and put an end to the war between the sexes. And then America will, perhaps, acquire the wisdom of older peoples and a spontaneity in regard to sex, arising out of that wisdom, without thereby sacrificing the specific character of its great and unique social experiment.

Some psychologists and moralists are already warning against the overdose of rationalism which their predecessors prescribed for American families. Dr. Alexander Reid Martin, the psychiatrist, sees the roots of sexual disturbances in the cold reasonableness with which parents believe they should enlighten their children regarding the facts of life (around the age of seven). This, says the doctor, is a monumental error, and he prefers Victorian prudishness: "I am absolutely sure that all the prissiness of the Victorian era, with the children whispering among themselves and sneaking the home medical book for consultation and parents blushing and coughing at embarrassing questions, did more to invest sex with the delicacy that belongs to it than our clinical, casual, detached frankness." And in *The Decline and Fall of Sex,* Robert E. Fitch maintains that sexuality in America has en-

tered the ice age. Sex, he writes, "used to be hot stuff, but
now it smokes like a piece of dry ice." It has been reduced
to an "animal allure." And Fitch continues: "By the time
the modern intelligence is through with it, what sex gives
us is not a burn but a frostbite. It isn't wicked any longer,
and it isn't any fun. It's just biologic . . . This new intelligence
has assassinated sex."

Where, then, is the remedy? Perhaps in the Twist, since the
winter of 1961-62; "the brave new whirl," as Professor Marshall Fishwick has dubbed the new dance. He defends it as
"a valid manifestation of the Age of Anxiety; an outward
manifestation of the anguish, frustration and uncertainty of
the 1960's; an effort to release some of the tension which, if
suppressed and buried, could warp and destroy. In our dancing . . . we show who we are, and what America is in the
twentieth century."

But one cannot always be dancing the Twist, especially after
one has passed a certain age.

Attitude toward sex is after all only the expression of a
still deeper dilemma: modern man's relation to the sphere of
the instinctive, the unconscious, which seems in some way to
be disturbed—not only in America, but in all sophisticated
societies. But in America it is more apparent, because here
everything comes under the spotlight of publicity. Walter Kerr,
the drama critic, asks, in *The Decline of Pleasure* (1962),
how the paradox between the unpuritanical approval of the
pleasures of sex in modern life and its literary representation
is to be explained: "In the course of asserting the dignity and
the desirability of a natural act, we have been understandably
eager to free our art forms from the artificial silences imposed
by Victorianism so that they would come to reflect our own
new honesty and our own new joy. We have freed them. But
the reflection is most strange. What do our novels and plays
show back to us? Almost without exception an image of sex

that is violent, frustrated, shabby, furtive, degrading, treacherous and—more and more—aberrant."

The remedy he prescribes is based on one root of this disorder, which is also apparent to the European observer of love in the United States, and that is the loss of spontaneity: "the degree to which ordinarily spontaneous, outgoing, instinctive responses are at the mercy of a mind that has reached a controlling conclusion: the conclusion that all value resides in the abstract ratios, the theoretical equations, of our cerebral manipulation of things, and that no value is to be discovered by merely playful contact with the things themselves, whether those things be stone or salt water or flesh."

That is the root of the trouble. And the remedy? Again we agree with Walter Kerr: "Until the mind can be convinced that pleasure is meaningful, until it can feel that pleasure is just, until it can quite simply and plainly be pleased with itself, there will be no cakes and ale for anybody."

To be complex and simple at one and the same time, that may be a hard lesson to learn; in fact, it cannot be "learnt." But this may well be the key to the problems we have been discussing here.

8.

The Powerful Pictures

TELEVISION, an invention of applied technology—one is sometimes inclined to forget that it is not an autonomous demonic power—has wrought deeper changes in American society than any other invention with the exception of the automobile.

The mere dimensions of the television phenomenon are breath-taking. After a halting start in 1941, when the first licenses were issued, the electronic revolution began in earnest between 1947 and 1948. From 100,000 sets, production rose in a single year to one million. Now, in 1962, over fifty-five million sets are in use (compared with seven million in England, 1.5 million in the Soviet Union, and one million in West Germany). One hundred and fifty million Americans are regular TV viewers. Only the natural force of sleep is able to claim more time than TV from the American people as a whole. Television takes first place after sleep, with 2.6 billion hours a week—more than the two billion work hours in all branches of the economy. Children spend an average of three to four hours a day before the television screen, and to the dismay of their helpless parents, are furnished with daily prescriptions for murder, by westerns and crime stories. The average American adult—a statistical myth, but one which is probably very close to reality—watches television sixteen hours a week, or two hours and some minutes daily. On week days, he spends less time before the screen, but long hours on Sundays, when programs are far superior. Eighty-five per cent of all households have one or more TV sets (radio, with a ninety-six per cent ownership, has virtually reached saturation point).

In 1960, industry spent $1.6 billion on television advertising, an increase of 939 per cent over 1950. In the same year, the three major networks made profits approaching the one hundred million dollar mark. The American people has invested, in all, some twenty-five billion in television sets and services. As much money is spent on television and radio repairs as on theater, concerts, opera, and books combined.

The economic power of television does not consist exclusively in the enormous expenditure it involves, although the total of four billion dollars annually expended on electronically produced pictures and sound, around eight per cent of the gigantic defense budget of the United States, is certainly impressive. Its principal power, whereby it attracts the "sponsors" —as the advertisers are somewhat optimistically termed—lies in its contact with the consumer, which is carried practically to the point of taste and smell. The creation of needs through commercials, which the multi-million army of viewers has to put up with, has become one of the permanent driving forces of the affluent society, founded on the incessant production of goods. That is why the American gets his television programs for nothing.

The decision in favor of free television, which determines the structure of the industry more than any other single factor, was not arrived at by the networks on their own. It was taken out of their hands because radio, in the thirties, had definitely developed as a commercial, that is, in a twofold sense, *free* medium: free in the sense of independence of the State, and free in the sense of unpaid. The air waves were to be exploited by private capital. There is government regulation, of course, but only through the issuance of licenses, not through the influencing of programing. But it is under-

stood that the cession of a public domain—the air waves—
to the stations obligates them, at least on occasion, to perform
a public service. The stations exercise their magic power over
the air without government control. To give government
agencies any say in radio or television is still unthinkable to
Americans. And the principle of private exploitation is un-
affected even by the attempts that are made to avoid the tor-
ture of the commercials—the announcer's voice, always
several degrees too loud, praising tantalizing products, the
Disney-style cartoons, with their flying beer bottles, bursting
cans of tempting foods, singing cough drops and steaming
coffee. The commercials have to contend with a bored or
irritated public, who want to get back to the program as
quickly as possible and therefore regard them as an intrusion; hence the almost hysterical tone, the extravagant word-
ing with which the unwilling viewers are attacked.

The authors of the formulae which the announcers declaim
in tones of entreaty, hearty familiarity or deliberate casualness,
as the occasion requires, and which are supposed to influence
the degree of the consumer's needs, are often young men who
have studied philosophy and literature at expensive colleges.
They have been called the foreign legion of desperate minds,
hiring out their services to the hectic world of advertising. But
the advertising formulae which interrupt the atmosphere of
a Thornton Wilder play or a fairy tale are not interlopers in
this system. For the firms concerned have, after all, bought
time on the screen; it belongs to them. They finance the trans-
mission and are therefore entitled to interrupt it with their
commercials.

The television networks do not sell time as such, but time
plus audience—for what really interests industry is the viewers,
the potential consumers, in the greatest possible numbers. The
larger the audience a television program can offer, the more
expensive will be the time which the network sells with it
to the sponsor. Inevitably, therefore, the goal is to ensure

as broad an audience as possible. Only for a potential buying public running into the millions is the industrial sponsor prepared to purchase one of the increasingly expensive television programs, which is then transmitted in his name, so that he, in turn, will be enabled to sell as much as possible of his particular product, be it cars or cosmetics, cigarettes, soap, beer, refrigerators or aspirin tablets.

The disadvantages of this system of commercial television are obvious. The search for the common denominator of taste among the greatest number cannot promote quality; the most ardent democrat would not suggest that it did. A leveling down is almost unavoidable. Tolerance becomes insipidity, as nobody's susceptibilities must be offended. In a conflict between controversy and conformity, the desire to please the greatest number will always weight the decision in favor of the latter. For the sponsor there are "sacred cows" that must not be touched, particularly in matters of race, sex, party politics and religion. There is thus an employer's veto. The industrial concern which purchases a program, through its publicity and sales experts thus exerts a tacit influence on its content.

Now that the depth psychologists have been drawn into the advertising business and exploit—or profess to exploit—social taboos or the father complex or the urge for security for advertising purposes, the publicity experts who spend hundreds of thousands of dollars for programs will also try, by means of the screenplay in between the commercials, to make the viewer unconsciously susceptible to opinions coinciding with the interests of the sponsor. An insurance company, for example, will hardly recommend that one risk one's life on the barricades.

The arbiter which determines whether the television producer is to be or not to be, is the statistical opinion poll, an institution as inhuman as its results are questionable. Four special services exist, also very highly paid for by the sponsors, to check whether a program is worth the hundreds of thousands of dollars invested in it. The rating produced by these special services is based on the size of the viewing public. If the size of an audience declines, the program disappears from the TV market in as meteoric a fashion as it may first have appeared, and with it the producers, script writers, directors and stage managers involved.

The operative principle is opinion sampling. One hundred million persons cannot be questioned, but one or two thousand can. Different methods are used. There are the audimeters connected with sets which mechanically register which of the twelve channels is being used. Or a thousand sample telephone calls are made; or individuals who are supposed to constitute a representative cross-section of the public are asked to take daily notes on their viewing.

Ratings have become the dubious crutches on which the television industry moves in the impasse of its own making—that of having to measure art quantitatively, to establish the link between performance and an invisible public scattered in forty-five million homes (a problem so easily handled through the theater box office). So far, despite the understandable distaste of artists and program producers for the ordeal of the fortnightly program rating, no other system has yet been evolved. And so long as figures indicate success, there will be no other. It belongs to commercial television as human sacrifice belonged to barbaric religion.

But, in any case, only a minority of Americans would like to give up the existing structure of radio and television in favor of a system where viewers would pay for the programs they watch, in other words, a system independent of the commercial sponsor. It is an intellectual minority; but the electronic revolution is a mass phenomenon in which the minority, as in all revolutions, can prevent its own exclusion only if it places itself at the head of the movement. There is room enough for it, as we shall see. Only one thing is no longer possible: to ignore the power of television. For the individual, if he likes, it is not inescapable; we are not yet in Orwell's world. But in society as a whole, the intrusion of television into the living room, and the resulting familiarity with sights and sounds and social symbols from New York or Hollywood, constitute a second reality in the intimate sphere of the home such as no technical instrument of entertainment has ever before been able to produce.

So far, the attempts to introduce pay television have been in vain. It may therefore be assumed that the structure of television will remain commercial, that is, in the hands of private capital. At any rate, there is no question of government agencies or public-chartered institutions taking over the direction of television. The American would rather put up with commercials than accept any such official intervention. The question is whether the quality of the programs can be improved by freeing them from the shackles of the commercial sponsor; this could be done by licensing new stations independent of advertising alongside the three major networks with their affiliated local stations (some five hundred of them). The three major networks (CBS, NBC, ABC) are fearful of any challenge to their concentrated, if rival, power, and have therefore succeeded in preventing the emergence of pay television. Their most common argument is that subscription television would take their best programs away; artists and producers would desert them. The argument has doubtful merit, since the prospect of an audience of millions, which only the three giant New York companies could offer, must be a tempting one to any performer. Commercial television will remain the dominant form simply because it is an expression of the mobile, "Carthaginian" society which trusts in the forces of the market and is constantly stimulated by them.

Then there is also the nexus of interests. Oddly enough, the tentative licensing of pay television, which was supposed

to take place for the first time in 1958, was blocked. Lobbies
of the powerful television industry succeeded in getting congressional committees to take the matter out of the hands of
the Federal Communications Commission which issues licenses.
The link between congressmen and local television is almost
inevitable; television has become vital for every election campaign, and some members of Congress are themselves co-
owners of local stations, whose political power may already
exceed that of the local press.

In 1962, there began in Hartford, Connecticut, a three-year
experiment in pay-TV (conducted by RKO—General Phone-
vision). About forty hours weekly of programing may be
received by subscribers who will have decoders attached to
their TV sets to "unscramble" the pay TV signals. This is the
battle of the coin-in-the-slot channel against free channels. The
outcome of the experiment is altogether uncertain, but it does
present the public with the opportunity of watching quality
performances—legitimate theater, opera, ballet, concerts, and
other events—without interruptions by irritating commercials.
In any case, such experiments are welcome if only because
they force the commercial stations to adopt higher standards.

But it would be illusory to imagine that because television
is operated by private enterprise it can live on some abstract
plane, untouched by politics or covert manipulations of influence and wealth. The connecting link between the business
of politics and the sphere of electronic picture magic is the
regulatory agency, the Federal Communications Commission.
The physical fact that wave lengths cannot be used without
limitation led, in 1927, to the creation of an official radio
commission. Its importance increased enormously with television, so that the FCC, as a Senate investigation has revealed,
has become a hotly contested focal point of political pressure,
bureaucratic power, and money interests.

Newspaper publishers who want to open a broadcasting
station will often constitute a legally sanctioned monopoly

thanks to their license. If they obtain the increased financial power they seek, they may also be in a position to eliminate local newspaper competitors. The result is a concentration of power which the FCC, under its terms of reference, is supposed to prevent. Or representatives and senators support TV stations. The members of the FCC know that the Senate has to approve all important nominations, and it may be useful for one's future career to have friends there. All this is almost inevitable, and only confirms how deeply television —despite the mantle of private enterprise which it wears— reaches into the political power structure of the country and is influenced by it.

With the nomination by the Kennedy Administration of the fearless Newton N. Minow as Chairman of the FCC, a new era of regulatory activity has opened. (One even hears of "Minowism.") The new chairman began his official career by calling television "a vast wasteland," and has since inspired in the executives of the mass media a healthy anxiety regarding quality. As Jack Gould of the *New York Times* wrote about Minow's first year in office: "Into the arena of public opinion he has projected a second contender—the agency to protect the public interest in broadcasting—as a factor to be reckoned with in charting the home medium's future course . . . In the world of television, he has introduced a more realistic system of checks and balances between industry and government." His most perceptible influence is in the field of TV journalism, which since 1961 has evidenced a greater advance than any other field of programing. Robert Kennedy, who should know, called the first Kennedy-Nixon television debate "the single most important factor in the entire 1960 campaign." A greater tribute to the power of TV is hardly conceivable.

Is television an art? In the first place, the electronic tube is a means of transportation, basically little different from the automobile (with which it shares the position of exerting a tremendous influence on a people's way of life). It is a neutral instrument for the conveyance of pictures and sounds. Whether this instrument is used to create a new art form and whether it is placed at the service of intelligent expression, are human decisions. It offers great artistic possibilities, and it has its limitations. But the hypnotic power of the screen, the possibilities for dulling escapism offered by television more than any other medium, are not inevitable. A mere turn of the knob immediately breaks the spell. A selective attitude to the knob on the television set is the answer to most complaints by intellectuals. In the invention as such, there is no inherent demonic or bewitching power. The television tube itself, obviously should be regarded as outside of both good and evil.

The greatest limitation on standards is the time factor. An unbelievable amount of time has to be filled with programs, without any interruption. There simply cannot be so much quality as to provide a single network with good programs five thousand hours a year, eighteen hours a day, seven times a week, with hardly a minute's silence. (The whole Hollywood movie industry produces six hundred hours of film a year.) Hence the Moloch-like consumption of talent, which Red Skelton has called "the glass furnace," constantly burning up material.

American television is the great catalyst which brings together all the other forms of art and information—comedians and singers, journalists and professors, dancers and teachers, film actors, circus and cabaret performers, preachers and sportsmen, theater, ballet, short films, documentaries, up-to-the-minute reporting, quiz shows, parlor games, and debates. All these are forms borrowed from other media, but at the same time adapted to the esthetic rules of this particular medium. The insatiability of the time that has to be filled, combined with the sponsor's desire to secure his investment, have this consequence: the gigantic mixture is standardized into a few types, and "trends" are created by the rating process. The great rival studios develop these trends by following every taste fluctuation of the public like an imperious oracle.

For nearly ten years, the comedians were the kings of TV: Milton Berle, who indulged in slapstick and pie-throwing, spoke in a shrill falsetto, and danced in female attire; Jackie Gleason, who played comic parts with a human touch reminiscent of Chaplin; Sid Caesar, a caustic satirist, who with his partner, Imogene Coca, poked fun at the Hollywood movie personalities.

Then came the trend in favor of musical entertainers, around whom sumptuous shows were created: Liberace, Perry Como, Arthur Godfrey, Lawrence Welk ("Champagne Music") and, of course, Frank Sinatra. (Programs like "Sing Along With Mitch" perpetuate this trend through the present.) Their attraction was surpassed by the westerns, films of pioneering days, among them masterpieces of their genre, in which desperadoes do not step on the gas but still ride horseback, as does the ever courageous sheriff: real horse operas. For westerns and mysteries together are part of the cult of violence so astonishingly omnipresent in American life.

The new role in television which has fallen to Hollywood's lot is not unjustly held responsible for the profit-seeking, mediocrity, standardization, fear of bold experiment, and loss of reality which bedevil television, at a time when it is achieving increasing technical perfection. So far, artistic quality has developed in inverse ratio to the expansion of the medium. Only a revolt of the public—and there are a number of indications that such a revolt is in the making—can halt this decline.

The public's appetite for searing reality on TV was demonstrated in the grotesquely misguided popularity of the quiz shows. Every night, thousands of dollars were bestowed by advertisers on men, women, and children laboring, apparently, under varying degrees of nervous strain, as they answered questions requiring an astonishing photographic memory. The proceedings were conducted in an almost ritual format. Charles Van Doren, a lecturer at Columbia University, became a national figure; an eleven-year-old scientific prodigy won $200,000; a policeman turned out to be an expert on Shakespeare, a shoemaker an expert on opera. The prospect of watching a man painfully wrestling with his memory and finally giving up, as he inevitably must, and scrutinizing his features in close-up as he does so, constituted one of the attractions of these thought tournaments, which ultimately turned out to be such cruel deceptions.

After the quiz scandals of 1959 (in which Van Doren was only a prototype) the discredited shows disappeared. Now, however, not so long after, they have re-emerged under the heading of "game" shows, which fill the mornings of the viewing housewife.

As with the film, whose greatest days were those when it was technically clumsiest, so with television, people talk nostalgically of a "golden age"—around the years 1950-1954—when creative experiments in television theater were being attempted and a number of young authors, actors and directors collaborated in shaping the new esthetic content of the young medium. Many small, one-hour television dramas were hopeful beginnings, which were developed by a whole series of programs. Productions like Thornton Wilder's *The Bridge of San Luis Rey* proved the possibility of an independent TV art, differing from the related art forms of theater and film by traits peculiar to it alone: intimacy, residing both in the intrusion of the scene in the viewer's home and in intensive optical and aural closeness which lends itself to subtle tones, nuances, atmosphere; and emphasis on a section of the picture in which a detail or a marginal event can suddenly become the channel of feeling, bound up with the spoken word, and unexpectedly taking the principal role.

Much the most convincing TV drama so far has been the adaptation of Wilder's novel centered around the death of five people on a hanging bridge in Peru (two previous film versions are considered failures). Here, in an extraordinary feat of direction, the TV medium proved superior. The telecast on CBS—live, not on film—cost several hundred thousand dollars, paid for by Du Pont. It will never be possible to estimate whether Thornton Wilder's metaphysical play contributed to the increased sale of nylon thread. But the production was a brilliant justification of private television. Very big firms will always be prepared to finance important artistic schemes for reasons of prestige. Almost half the public to whom the telecast was available saw Thornton Wilder's play that evening.

Fortunately there are occasionally other such high spots, as for instance, in 1961, Graham Greene's *The Power and the Glory* produced by David Susskind. But one of the sad aspects of contemporary television is that live network drama "is virtually dead, killed by tape and film," as John Bartlow Martin complains. The writer once rose at 5:30 a.m. to look at channel 5 for twenty continuous hours. "At last, at 1:52 a.m., all became darkness." After this ordeal he asked himself: "Why is so much of television so bad? Why is some so good?" That is truly the unresolved antinomy of television.

The television hypnosis is diminishing; people are becoming more selective. The curve depicting mass TV viewing time no longer rises. The electronic revolution has now been in progress for over ten years, and, like all revolutions, its impetus is slowing. It is quite possible that the electronic pictures will cease to exert such power. This prospect is a healthy antidote to complacency of the medium, and could serve as a spur to higher quality, for television still possesses great untapped reserves of quality. In the language of numbers, Shakespeare's *Romeo and Juliet* was seen by twelve million persons, *Richard III*, with Laurence Olivier, by fifteen million viewers. In this way more people experienced Shakespeare in a few hours than in the centuries since he first wrote his plays.

A special sphere of television, which so far has been developed primarily only in children's programs (a substantial part of over-all programing) is a kind of playful surrealism, the delightful fairy story fantasy. Even adults could enjoy Shirley Temple's "Story Book" and "Walt Disney's World." If there is a future for television, it lies in these two extremes: in the purely imaginary and in the communication of the immediate, the exploitation of a unique capacity to bring the realities of the here and now into the privacy of the home.

There is a saying that in television nothing is black and white save the picture on the screen. Just as the tremendous variations in programs make it impossible to generalize about standards, so the dictum that TV has a series of inviolable taboos also allows of exceptions. Mike Wallace, for instance, a young intellectual born in New York of Russian immigrants, has no fear of controversy. His invention was the ruthlessly revealing thirty-minute interview in which the interviewee—nearly always someone well known—deliberately exposed himself (or herself) to the danger of having the excellently prepared interviewer put his finger on some hidden wound. His program did not survive, but, in 1962, he returned to the screen with "P.M. Report." In this program he uses a more moderate form of his discussion technique, with several guests at once, rather like Susskind's "Open End," and—again like Susskind—shows that endless patience with which Americans are able to follow the meandering stream of improvized debate.

Surrealism is one pole of TV, reality the other. To quote Minow, "TV is more than an advertising medium, more than a competitor for newspapers and magazines. If TV doesn't present reality, how can we deal with life in the '60's?"

Political events and the continuous crises which have made the United States increasingly conscious of its ties with the

rest of the world, have encouraged the trend toward more
and better TV journalism. This trend reached a high point
in the 1961-62 season, with ABC's "Closeups," Brinkley's
"Journal" (on NBC), "CBS Reports," and CBS' "The
Twentieth Century" and "Eyewitness" (in both of which
Walter Cronkite was the narrator).

The most gifted journalist on TV was Edward R. Murrow,
who now heads the United States Information Agency. He
made a name with his radio reports from London during
the Blitz. His television documentaries on crises in different
parts of the world, and his reports on social problems at
home, have a distinctive style (not unmarred by mannerism)
which can be traced back to the breathless intensity of those
wartime broadcasts. In March, 1954, disregarding the rule of
political neutrality, Murrow presented a program on Mc-
Carthy, in which he let the Senator himself speak, in film
excerpts from committee hearings. There could have been
no more effective condemnation of the man—and it required
a great deal of civic courage at the time to attack the anti-
Communist McCarthy before millions of eyes. Murrow
evidenced similar courage in his report on prostitution, which
provoked consternation among his viewers. He had prostitutes
describe the widespread big-business practice of offering "call-
girls" as a service to customers, upon the signing of a contract.

Five years after the McCarthy program, the same Edward
R. Murrow bitterly denounced his own medium: "To a very
considerable extent the media of mass communications in a
given country reflect the political, economic and social climate
in which they flourish . . . We are currently wealthy, fat,
comfortable and complacent. We have currently a built-in
allergy to unpleasant or disturbing information. Our mass
media reflect this. But unless we get up off our fat surpluses
and recognize that television in the main is being used to
distract, delude, amuse and insulate us, then television and
those who finance it, those who look at it and those who

work at it, may see a totally different picture too late." Here Murrow refers to the danger that television might become obsolescent. "This instrument can teach, it can illuminate; yes, and it can even inspire. But it can do so only to the extent that humans are determined to use it to those ends. Otherwise it is merely wires and lights in a box."

Murrow has had no successors in such fearless handling of controversial themes, with the possible exception of the NBC White Paper on the U-2 incident, which appeared late in 1961. Murrow was a pioneer of what optimistic analysts of the medium call its new "journalism phase."

The 1959 quiz scandals were a signal for a reappraisal of television, with a view to halting the decline in quality resulting from the commercialism which penetrated virtually every facet of the industry. American society is sometimes called "imitative." But there is reason to believe that the imitative urge can also be used for the greater good of this unfinished society. Quality will find imitators, for it is not ability that is lacking, only the will to take action. Thus, Walter Lippmann suggests the establishment of a network of stations which would be freed from the tyranny of the profit motive by endowments and public subsidies, after the manner of the principal universities, hospitals, space exploration and basic research projects. This network, operated in the public interest, would serve as a model and standard of intellectual quality for the privately owned television industry. Congressman Henry Reuss, from Wisconsin, has proposed that the television industry be obliged to make contributions from its enormous profits to finance cultural and educational programs of high quality. The stations would then have to transmit them as a public service and without advertising fees. Both proposals, arising out of the quiz scandals, point in the same direction: the restraint of private interests by the injection of the public interest. In this sense, the reform of television will be a part of the self-correcting process of capitalism.

There is still little consensus about the philosophical questions of television: what *is* television—a medium of art, a device to sell more goods, or a shortcut to spiritual oblivion? What is its aim? It came into being as a technical invention, but its nature transcends mechanics. American television may, in the future, change the environment of civilization, and it could, at the same time, lose some of its power over human beings and lower its quality more and more. In this sense, TV seems to be at the crossroads.

Perhaps the key lies in the way in which this youngest of the mass media relates to reality. This question has two dimensions: first, how real are the pictures themselves? And, secondly, how is the national consciousness of reality affected by the unique phenomenon of some one hundred million people daily spending hours in idleness, absorbed in television images and sounds?

The first part of the question is rather easily dealt with. As mentioned before, TV is at its best at the two poles of programing (imaginative plays and visual reporting). In terms of metaphysical definition, this means that television is enjoyment, indulgence, and fantasy, as well as education and information. It is both escapism and realism, this seeming dichotomy being not really unusual. Indeed, it is to be found in most creations of the human mind. The danger might lie in distinguishing the different levels of reality, in maintaining a healthy perspective.

This danger points to what might be the fundamental question for television: How does the ceaseless cataract of images affect the sense of reality of the viewers?

In a book, *The Obsolescence of Man,* published some time ago in Germany, Gunther Anders propounds the thesis that the viewer loses the sense of reality, even the sense of his own reality. The pictures transmitted on television are phantoms, he maintains, because they are both there and not there. In terms of identification with the screen images, the viewer will eventually become a phantom too. If this is true, it is indeed a craven capitulation to a mechanical-electronic device of our own making, warped into something diabolical. However, even the addicted American TV viewer is much too familiar with the mechanics of this electronic picture world to go completely overboard. As a member of a self-critical, mobile society, he has gradually become suspicious of attempts to manipulate him and is, therefore, rather immune to the danger of becoming the unwitting victim of a phantom world.

The contrary is more liable to occur: that every reality shown on the TV screen will be regarded as phantom. Reality on TV might thus lose its credibility. In self-defense, the viewers could be induced to a protectively shed illusion. As images race over the screen, alternately bringing messages of courage, justice, love, crime, jello, or deodorants, all with the same fervor, the effect could easily be a "disassociation" from all the reality presented. Although it is most unlikely that the masses of viewers will become as "hip" as the beatniks, who would not be caught dead in front of a television set, it could lead to increasing disillusionment with the medium.

It is basic to man to be able to operate on different levels of reality, a fact considerably older than the invention of the electronic tube. In a primitive society, based on magic, the second reality of the TV screens could well become the dominating phantoms Gunther Anders fears. But it is no coincidence that nuclear fission and the electronic revolution were born so close together in time. A society which technologically has become endlessly sophisticated fosters a type of person which, to survive, strengthens certain characteristics and sheds others. This human type may have lesser roots in a native soil, but he will frequently be capable of vicarious experience of understanding imagination, and will have some recognition of the broad variety of human expression.

He will not become schizophrenic just by watching "The

Twilight Zone." But if all the reality that is offered to the viewer seems to be in the spiritual twilight, he might become uninterested. The future of television—of the "vision which comes from afar"—will ultimately be directly related to the degree to which it aids human beings to live in a complex society—not by offering them only an escapist stupor, but by entertaining with grace and wit and informing with honesty. Now, at the crossroads, which direction will be taken?

9.

The Bypassing of Equality

GEORGETOWN may be called the mother of the federal capital of Washington, D.C. It has long since become a mere section of the capital city, but at the same time, it is known as "the most powerful village in the world." Unique historical flavor is there, linked here with an intensely immediate present: Society (with a capital S) linked with political power. Not everyone who lives in Georgetown is influential, but an unusual number are; hardly anywhere else will one find so many members of the social and political elite of a world power center living together in an area of a couple of square miles.

For over thirty years, now, the Episcopal church of St. John's, in Georgetown, has been organizing a quite exceptional ritual around Easter time. For the benefit of St. John's the doors of the most beautiful houses are opened to the public, and in a vernal procession, incomprehensible to the uninitiated, one sees small groups of people walking through the length and breadth of Georgetown, disappearing inside houses and gardens and then reappearing again. Inside, gracious ladies instruct them in English Regency and Gothic styles, Queen Anne furniture, chinoiseries, dull silver and Bohemian glassware, ornaments on high mantels, old family portraits in oil, collections of moderns like Dufy, Derain and Rouault (but no abstract painters), the art of dried flower arrangement and, in general, about the charm of the eighteenth century here preserved.

The cult of esthetic living must be observed. Consequently, the white doors of the porticos with their brightly polished brass knobs, set between classical columns surmounted by arches, or simply surrounded by a gay molding, are closed by the colored butler so that they may again perform their normal function, namely, to seclude the political Society of the American capital, with gentle discretion, from the outside world.

It is perhaps too much to say that to understand America one has to understand Georgetown. For what is Georgetown, after all, but a collection of old houses and select antiquities? It has been likened to Mayfair in London because it is the socially right address, or to Montparnasse, because artists' studios and picture galleries lend it a deceptively artistic note. But in reality, Georgetown is an unmistakably American phenomenon.

In the seventeenth century, a hinterland of rich plantations built itself a harbor on the Potomac in order to ship tobacco crops from Maryland. Like Charleston in the South, the town houses of Georgetown were soon the scene of a brilliant social culture. As early as 1775, the English General Braddock wrote home: ". . . never have I attended a more complete banquet, or met better dressed or better mannered people than I met on my arrival in George Town, which is named after our gracious Majesty."

In 1791, the first President of the United States, the aristocratic general from neighboring Virginia, founded the capital that bears his name on an empty and marshy site ten miles square. At the time, and for a number of decades after, Georgetown regarded itself as superior to Washington in elegance, comfort and tradition. But eighty years later it had declined almost completely into a Negro slum. However, the intelligent, esthetically perceptive young men from Harvard and Princeton, whom President Roosevelt brought to Washington in 1933, looked with understanding eyes at the classical façades of the Federal style which had marked Georgetown architecture between 1775 and 1825. Roosevelt's "brain trust" rediscovered Georgetown and "rehabilitated" it. Today, there are still two hundred Federal buildings, and they still determine the atmosphere of the section, even though most of the houses are Victorian.

If Georgetown, situated just over half a mile from the White House, can claim a philosophy of life of its own, then it is a very conservative one. Thoughtful conversations on the ivy-covered patio, political discussion in front of an open fire or by candlelight at a dinner party, the cult of antique furniture, libraries of books reaching up to the ceiling, withdrawal to the intimate and traditional—all these enter into that philosophy.

In Georgetown, the eighteenth century still projects into the living style of those who wield present-day power. The present President of the United States lived in this section; the first Kennedy Cabinet was constituted in his small, high town house on N Street. Georgetown is a civic symbol of the unexpected role which tradition plays just under the surface of American life. A part of this role is played by Society; it is no insignificant role, however hard this may be to understand—much harder to grasp than the place of the architecture of 1775, which is protected under the Act for the Preservation of American Antiquities.

Life must have been delightful in eighteenth-century Virginia, the oldest English colony on the East Coast of the New World. Barely one hundred years after the first settlers, in 1607, had built their sedge huts in Jamestown (where most of them perished of privation), a planter aristocracy had developed in Virginia which adapted the style of life of the English landed gentry to the tobacco plantations of this green and spacious countryside, watered by a thousand streams.

The Negro slave, however, was a non-English institution,

as was the larger scale of things. The tobacco planters achieved rapid wealth, thanks to land grants. Their mansions, supported by tall, white, wooden columns, always lay near the water; they had their own quays, and the boats which loaded the tobacco bales returned with Negro slaves from Africa and with luxury goods—clothing and choice furniture, the things which belong to the life of gentry—from London. For despite the endless expanse of ocean which separated them from England, these families felt themselves close to the capital and not at all a colonial province. A report dated 1724 states: "Any Thing may be delivered to a Gentleman there from London, Bristol, &c. with less Trouble and Cost than to one living five Miles in the Country in England; for you pay no Freight for Goods from London . . ."

By 1750, the social structure of Virginia had consolidated into a planter aristocracy, patriarchally governing its extensive estates, Negro slaves and white artisans. It was a regime far removed from the egalitarian notion of equal opportunities for all. Barely more than one hundred families ruled the wealthy colony—the "best families," who intermarried and shut themselves off against new immigrants, for whom there was in any case little free land left. They were also the political masters, thus constituting a caste comparable to the European nobility, an untitled aristocracy "founded on smoke"—on tobacco—and far too anxious to emulate the ideal of the English gentleman to be described as a vulgar, monied, ruling class.

These families, together, ruled Virginia like a single big plantation. (Of the ninety-one men whom the Governor called to the House of Burgesses between 1680 and 1775, the beginning of the War of Independence, almost two-thirds belonged to only twenty-three families.) They were the first manifestation of an American Society, in which wealth, and power based on wealth, combine in a recognized upper class, a Society which can unhesitatingly be written with a capital initial to distinguish it from the rest of mankind. Seventeenth and eighteenth century names are still proof of membership in one of Virginia's "old families," even without a planter aristocracy or Negro slaves (but servants)—names like Byrd, Page, Lee, Ludwell, Wormeley, Carter, Harrison, Randolph and, a little later, Jefferson and Washington.

Here we have what is, perhaps, the most deep-seated paradox in the emergence of America. The "Virginia dynasty" of the first presidents of the independent federal State—Washington, Jefferson, Madison and Monroe—came from precisely this planter aristocracy. Within that aristocracy there developed the powers and the ideas which made the colonies independent of England and gave them a free, if conservative, domestic regime. The revolution against England was planned on the dignified estates on the banks of the Virginia streams. It was at Gunston Hall on the Potomac, in a classical mansion surrounded by strictly laid out paths lined with boxwood hedges, that George Mason drafted the declaration of human rights which was incorporated in the Federal Constitution as the Bill of Rights. The roots of American representative democracy plunge deep into the social soil of the old Virginian society, even if their flowering is very different from anything the traditionalist George Washington could have imagined.

It is fascinating to reflect how the selfsame roots could have brought forth both the American mass society and the first genealogical trees of Society. Perhaps this curious sociological dual root explains why, however much Society and its formerly uninhibited and ostentatious extravagance have been castigated, its actual existence has never been called into question or regarded as incompatible with the character of the United States as a political democracy.

"When the United States ceased to be a greater Virginia, Virginians ceased to govern the United States," writes the historian, Daniel Boorstin. The self-assured lords of the plantation style of living were the leaders of the anti-English revolt; but their own economic world could not long survive the collapse of English rule. Except in the South, the upper class began to sever its ties with the soil and take on the leadership of an industrial and financial, economic society. This was the beginning, within Society, of the ceaseless conflict between old wealth and new.

When money made its appearance in such fantastic abundance as in the generation of the multimillionaires, it was simply not possible for the older families to forbid their entry into Society. But the doors were always quickly closed again. If Society is not exclusive, it soon ceases to be Society altogether. But a Society which has never had an hereditary aristocracy and whose standing, basically—though never exclusively—derives from economic power, finds it hard to justify its exclusiveness. That is why, in America more than anywhere else, the social upper crust is hedged about with a complex system of imponderables; devices have had to be found to make up for genealogy. Morality, religion, race, region, all play their part, however intangible. (Some of the tacit requirements are, for instance, that one should be of Anglo-Saxon origin, Protestant, not divorced, and not from Texas.) A European Almanac of Gotha is a children's primer compared with the Social Register of New York, Boston or New Orleans.

The old families, whose wealth dates back before 1860, and which have therefore been wealthy for three or four generations, enjoy undisputed social precedence. The very great fortunes, which made some Americans the richest men on earth, were only made with the industrialization of the country on a continental scale between the Civil War and the First World War. In the 1920's, before the Depression, there came into being the great automobile fortunes, and in the 'fifties, Texas, with its oil, became the cradle of the newest multimillionaires. But all this does not mean that there is, as it were, a plutocratic admission card to Society. The process is considerably more complex.

In New York Society—which, with Boston and Phila-delphia, represents the clearest embodiment of the type of big city "four hundred families"—the old families which can trace their descent back before 1860 were founded by Dutch or English immigrants who made local history by reason of their services to the community. They were people like Van Rens-selaer, Roosevelt, Remsen, Suydam, Van Cortlandt, Livingston, Barclay, Auchincloss, and Hamilton, and they constituted the old guard of New York Society. They were influential local elites who erected a wall of respectability about their personal lives. Life behind that wall had already become a little dull and formal, when it was seriously breached, in the last two decades of the nineteenth century, under the assault of a com-pletely different species of successful men.

The generation of multimillionaires, of entrepreneurs and financiers, who derived immense profits from the industrial revolution, promoted themselves to the status of a social aristocracy. They became Society leaders. This millionaire-Society of the turn of the century, with its often grotesque luxury, obscured the picture of the American upper class. The old families tended to look down on the *nouveaux riches,* but they could hardly ignore the enormous power these people had built up for themselves. The new rich simply grasped the social leadership thanks to the vast scope of their dollar power.

The conservative upper class tried, around 1900, to exclude the very rich newcomers from the "four hundred families," but they failed in their attempt. The newly rich forced them-selves through the eye of the social needle by firmly widening it. Only the designation "four hundred" remained, going back to the number of guests whom Mrs. Astor invited to her ball in 1892. The list of names which she drew up, together with Ward McAllister, a kind of master of ceremonies of the old Society, included only nine of the ninety richest families of the day. That list was subsequently replaced by the Social Register, which today lists thirty-eight thousand families for the whole of the United States. Meanwhile the "four hundred" in the cities with social traditions have become some four thousand, and the connection between Society and wealth is much closer than Mrs. Astor was willing to admit in her day. This is easy to understand from the structure of the economy. Wealth is coming to be founded increasingly on inherited wealth. And it is becoming increasingly unusual for anyone to rise to the millionaire class from the very bottom. At the present time, "self-made men" constitute only nine per cent of the highest income group; twenty-three per cent come from the middle class and sixty-eight per cent from an upper class that has long been wealthy. For the most part, this class has been able to maintain itself, despite depression, welfare State and progressive income tax, by merging with the giant corporations, even if it meant sharing the leadership with management. The corporations operate under impersonal names and, hence, obscure the names of the old families associated with them (except in cases like Du Pont). Today, one can speak of a self-perpetuation of Society, which has less and less to fear from the onslaught of new wealth and consequently is becoming more hidden and more exclusive.

The Astors (real estate), who migrated to New York in 1783 from Waldorf, regarded the Vanderbilts (railroads) as parvenus. But when Mrs. William Vanderbilt, who already belonged to the third generation since the founding of the first fortune, organized a fancy-dress ball in 1883, at a cost of $250,000, Mrs. William Astor decided reluctantly to leave her card at Mrs. Vanderbilt's so that her daughter, Caroline, might be invited.

The new multimillionaires stamped Society with that slightly absurd feudal style by which they hoped to outdo the European nobility, not only in wealth but in pomp and splendor. These industrial magnates, with their wives and daughters—"robber barons" to the social critics, but appreciated by the populace rather in the manner of a theatrical performance, as witness the social columns in contemporary newspapers—succeeded, by means of their parties and luxurious whims, in demonstrating to the world the naive novelty of their prosperity. The greatest names among them are Rockefeller (oil), Mellon (aluminum), Morgan (banking), Du Pont (munitions, chemicals), Gould (railroads), Harriman (railroads), Whitney (oil), Guggenheim (steel), Warburg (banking), and Winthrop (banking). In the 1920's the big automobile fortunes joined this top crust: Ford, Chrysler, Nash. Today it is the turn of the Texas oil millionaires. Three of them—J. Paul Getty, the richest and loneliest living American, as well as H. L. Hunt and Hugh Roy Cullen—have surpassed the billion-dollar mark, as only John D. Rockefeller, around 1900, and Henry Ford, around 1925, had done before them. The Texas fortunes form a contemporary epilogue to the long conflict between old and new money in Society. The successors of the millionaires, who prior to 1929 still lived their lives of "conspicuous consumption," have today become as conservative and reserved as Society was before the Civil War. They have lost the capacity of being rich naively.

Boston Society constitutes the closest approximation to an hereditary nobility. In *The Proper Bostonians,* Cleveland Amory describes the prototype of the American aristocrat. The "proper Bostonian" is a Protestant, of English descent, and like his father and grandfather before him has gone to Groton and then to Harvard. His fortune originated in shipping but is now largely derived from banking. He lives in the Beacon Hill section of Boston. He is more cultivated than his counterpart in New York, as becomes a descendant of those great Puritan men of letters, Emerson, Thoreau and Longfellow. He has never taken part in the excesses of ostentatious wealth, and his wife, for her part, has always preferred tweeds to mink.

Of the two first families, among the first families of Boston, the well-known saying goes that "the Lowells talk only to the Cabots, and the Cabots talk only to God." But in the fall of 1959, one of their number, Ambassador Cabot Lodge, had to talk for a week on end only to the atheistic Khrushchev, having been detailed to accompany him on his visit through the United States. For the proper Bostonians too, time does not stand still, as has been brought home to them by the loss of the municipal government to the Irish, none of whom, being non-English and Catholic, can claim real membership in Society.

In a subsequent book, Amory asks *Who Killed Society?,* and, in a joking vein, he lists under the indictment "Murder in the second degree" (based on "a poll of voters' preferences for the murderers of Society as of the 1960's"), the automobile, the telephone, the sputnik, and also "the Kennedy family." But for anyone who has lived in Washington, since a Bostonian became President, there can be no doubt of the accuracy of a different observation: "The New Frontier . . . has, first of all, returned Society's point of focus to the White House where it had not been for a number of years" (not, at least, since the days of Franklin D. Roosevelt).

Boston Society consists of concentric circles, the innermost of which is made up of the "first" families such as the Lowells, the Cabots, the Saltonstalls, the Cutlers, the Forbeses, the Adamses (who have given the United States two Presidents), the Frothinghams and the Gardners. Social newcomers may penetrate the outer circles—after efforts spanning perhaps no more than two generations—in the sense that they are invited to dinners, are permitted to sit on charitable committees and are even admitted to the Somerset Club. But the barrier falls when there is question of marriage. A girl who has attended the "right" schools may be invited, after she has excelled in an equestrian show, but that does not mean that her parents, too, are accepted in society; her daughters, however, will find things easier. Anyone concerned with the status which Society bestows has always had to think in terms of generations. This is a heritage of the way the nation grew out of the successive waves of immigration: the earlier arrivals were always a little more American than those who had just landed, so that mere existence in time confers a certain prestige, or at least it is often so regarded.

Philadelphia Society outdoes even the Brahmans of Boston in point of old and zealously guarded dignity. It too has found its portraitist. *Philadelphia Gentlemen,* by E. Digby Baltzell, bears the sub-title "The making of a national upper class." What he says about the "business aristocracy" of Philadelphia may therefore be applied to Society throughout the country. Traditionally, the members of Philadelphia Society live on Chestnut Hill (the old families have always chosen elevations in cities as their residential quarters). Their ancestors were Quakers of English or Welsh origin, who had distinguished themselves in the revolutionary years after 1776. In the nineteenth century, they became Episcopalians, which was more "refined" than being Quakers. Like themselves, their sons attend the Episcopalian boarding schools of New England reserved for scions of the upper classes, and then go on to Harvard, Yale, or Princeton. They belong to three clubs, which link them to the network of men's clubs in other cities, and they occupy the major posts in the big banks, the industrial enterprises, and the law firms of the city. But the municipal control, as in Boston, has slipped out of their hands.

There used to be a not very edifying connection between the financial upper class and corrupt municipal administrations, but such connections no longer appear to be the case. Society no longer provides much occasion for the kind of indignation which produced a spate of anti-Society literature in the thirties. The statement with which Ferdinand Lundberg opened his

America's Sixty Families, in 1937, could hardly seriously be made in the sixties: "The United States is owned and dominated today by a hierarchy of its sixty richest families, buttressed by no more than ninety families of lesser wealth . . . These families are the living center of the modern industrial oligarchy which dominates the United States, functioning discreetly under a *de jure* democratic form of government behind which a *de facto* government, absolutist and plutocratic in its lineaments, has gradually taken form . . . This *de facto* government is actually the government of the United States." In any case, the members of Society furnished abundant material for the astonishment of the masses and the indignation of the intellectuals. Their prototype was the eccentric New York Society, with its summer residences in Newport and Southampton, and its winter residences in Florida and on southern islands accessible only to their owners' yachts.

Today, the princely mansions of Newport, Rhode Island, which required staffs of hundreds of servants, are deserted. But in the golden age, at the turn of the century, there took place there, and in other Society mansions, the kind of things which Beard, who did not like the rich, described as follows: "At a dinner eaten on horseback, the favorite steed was fed flowers and champagne; to a small black and tan dog wearing a diamond collar worth $15,000 a lavish banquet was tendered; at one function, the cigarettes were wrapped in $100 bills; at another fine black pearls were given to the diners in their oysters . . . Then, weary of such limited diversions, the plutocracy contrived more freakish occasions—with monkeys seated between the guests, human goldfish swimming about in pools, or chorus girls hopping out of pies."

Barbara Hutton's parents gave a party at the Ritz-Carlton in New York at a cost of $100,000. The two thousand guests are supposed to have consumed one thousand cases of champagne. Debutantes' balls, produced like plays by famous directors, cost parents up to $250,000. At a wedding, five thousand chrysanthemums were painted dark pink to match the decorations on the wedding cake, which alone cost $2,000. The jewels, bathrooms, horses, private trains, cars (and then airplanes), not to mention the huge Wurlitzer organs which at night filled the gardens with music—all these were permanent themes in the press and were intended as such. Society was performing a duty to the masses by giving circuses; today that duty is performed by the magic pictures on the film strips and the television screens, together with the celebrities who appear on them.

Social Darwinism, that is, the doctrine that the most successful are also the smartest and the best, had long been a part of American popular belief—and served the rich as a self-justification. Consequently, the uninhibited exhibition of luxury was less offensive to the mass of the people than one might have thought. But a radical change in style came with the Depression of the thirties. It ended even the taste for "conspicuous consumption." Since then, refinement has again consisted in the absence of show.

The process of moral decontamination of excessive wealth began in the early years of the century—doubtless not uninfluenced by the introduction of the income tax in 1913— when the multimillionaires, led by Carnegie and Rockefeller, donated whole fortunes to philanthropic foundations. This association of elegance and charity is the formula whereby American Society, in a socially changed world, retains a public function which it is evidently reluctant to give up. For to attend select schools and universities, that is, to associate wealth (which others have, too, though mostly not for as long) with a certain type of culture, and thus to form ties with other well-educated and wealthy persons in order to cultivate a similar style of life, to invite certain persons and avoid others—all this certainly goes to make up the life of Society. But for the rest of the nation this life is largely invisible, being private. Yet, Society with a capital "S" still has a public function, as evidenced by the social columns in every newspaper.

Society derives its credentials from the Social Register, that mysterious tribunal which decides on the "to be or not to be," on the "in" or "out" of an individual in relation to Society. The Social Register was first published for New York and Boston in 1890. Now such lists of membership of Society appear in ten other cities: Philadelphia, Baltimore, Chicago, Washington, St. Louis, Buffalo, Pittsburgh, San Francisco, Cleveland, and Cincinnati. The advisers who determine this publication remain anonymous. No one knows exactly what criterion they employ to admit new names or—a decision liable to create a sensation—to strike names off. The Social Register of thirty-eight thousand names—mostly of married couples with their children, addresses, schools, and clubs—designates, according to its own words, "those families who by descent or by social standing or from other qualifications are naturally included in the best society of any particular city or cities."

This is very vague, as it cannot but be in America; nevertheless, the authority of the Social Register has never been seriously challenged within Society, and outside there is no question of any challenge, since so many apply for membership each year. The greatest effort in this direction is deployed by the managerial class of the big concerns, though there is, as yet, no evidence that money alone has ever secured a person's admission. There are always imponderables to be taken into account: schools, manners, connections, clubs—the exclusiveness of certain clubs can certainly vie with the exclusiveness of the Soial Register. One path through the needle's eye is by dint of strenuous endeavor, such as the socially ambitious woman who works her way up through her zeal in the organization of charitable works. C. Wright Mills, who could hardly be suspected of particular sympathy with the upper class, defended the Social Register as "an official status center that this country, with no aristocratic past, no court society, no truly capital city, possesses." Mills speaks of Society—apparently without conscious irony—as the "registered social class."

Only a small percentage of new names have been added to the Social Register—published anew each year—over the past few decades. But these interest the public less than the names that have been struck off. There have been quite astonishing inconsistencies in this respect. Sometimes a member is dropped because he has married an actress, whereas sometimes an actress is accepted after she becomes the wife of a "registered" member. Cornelius Vanderbilt Whitney was struck off after his divorce from the former Eleanor Seale, but her name remained on the list although she had been admitted only on the strength of her marriage. The membership of John Jacob Astor's widow was canceled after she married her son's boxing instructor. But John Hay Whitney, Ambassador to London under Eisenhower, himself applied to have his name removed from the Social Register because he considered the institution no longer in tune with the times, and Alfred Gwyne Vanderbilt did the same. Naturally, only members whose position is unassailable will take such action, since they do not need the Social Register anyway.

It has been said that notoriety, particularly through the press, is what turns the scale against a member, not the deeds leading to such notoriety. This point of view comes out in John O'Hara's *From the Terrace* (1958). He describes the attitude of an upper-class group, living in country houses on the North Shore of Long Island, with regard to love and divorce: "The presence of love was a cause of worry among the sisterhood. Individually they would aid and abet an affair that did not go beyond clandestine meetings for the pleasures of the body. But an affair that began as or became love, and threatened two marriages, was not to be encouraged . . . A man who allowed an illicit love to jeopardize his marriage and thereby to disturb good order forfeited what privileges he had. A similar punishment awaited the cuckolded husband who took his nasty discovery into the courts. He, too, had violated good order. One effect of this uncompromising attitude toward divorce and scandal was that it ironically gave a sense of security to wives who contemplated or were indulging in extra-marital affairs . . . This unsuspected immoral effect of an apparently highly moral prohibition might have been truly laughable had the keepers of good order established their rules as a moral code. But in reality, and although some of the keepers of good order were religious and sternly moral men, the purpose of good order and its enforcement was to keep the public in ignorance of the private lives of these men and their families."

For some ten years, now, the charity ball, however old-fashioned this institution may appear to Europeans, has become American Society's best weapon for killing many birds with one stone. Every winter season, hundreds of these balls take place in the expensive hotels of the country and net hundreds of thousands of dollars, which are used to assist orphans in Chicago, unmarried mothers in San Francisco, hospitals in New York, tsarist officers and Cuban art students, French, Greek, and Spanish welfare institutions, medical research, old-age homes, and countless other causes. Society ladies sit on committees which work for months on end in preparing these often extremely luxurious festivities. Here, of course, the members of Society are no longer among themselves, as they are, for instance, at the debutantes' balls for eighteen-year-old girls, who are introduced to Society with festivities representing something in the nature of worldly puberty rites. The object is to induce as many wealthy persons as possible to buy tickets to the balls, not only for themselves but for their guests—their "party." This is the way Society shows its power. The brilliance which it alone can lend to such gatherings is what prompts the expenditure of enormous sums for charitable purposes. In a single winter season in New York—and this is the social pattern in all the big cities—an average of ninety charity balls are held, bringing in some two million dollars, the contribution of "snob appeal" to a good cause.

Thus, morally secure, Society does not shun extravagance, though for private entertainment, funds on such a scale are no longer available, nor would good taste countenance their expenditure. But at an "April in Paris" ball in New York for the benefit of poor French children, some ten thousand dollars worth of French perfume may be sprayed around so that the air should smell of the Bois de Boulogne in spring.

Society thus entertains itself in a style which for itself it can no longer afford. The expenditures serve a "good cause" and thus give moral justification to this elegant extravagance; moreover, they are deductible from income tax. And in the thousandfold reflection of the social function which appears in the mass media of newspapers and magazines, films and television, Society sees itself as an integral part of the democratic society of the nation, a part that excludes but is not excluded, perhaps the most complex social phenomenon which American diversity has produced.

On the frontiers of "real" Society, there begin the social twilight zones of snobbery. The specifically American variant is the general seeking after personal "status," which Vance Packard discusses in *The Status Seekers* (1959). His sociopsychological analysis, after the manner of a deep-sea exploration, led to astonishing, if sometimes controversial, discoveries.

To the foreign observer, American life appears at first sight as egalitarian. He sees a colorful, vital, mobile surface, as compared with the old incrustations of European societies, which developed slowly. This surface is like an elevated plateau out of which there emerges an occasional mountain peak; the peak is not inconsistent with the plateau but rather confirms it. Everyone has the right to achieve pre-eminence, even if, in the nature of things, not everyone can do so. Some achieved it decades or centuries ago, and these consequently form the mountain peak of society. Under the surface, then, there unfolds a fascinating patchwork of consciously cultivated, group distinctions, involving not only a bewildering variety of snobberies, but also deeper forces of separation. The horizontal lines of income strata are intersected by other lines which can be called vertical, but also circular, in that the urge for separation is given effect in countless socially graduated clubs.

The result is a checker-board-like pattern of society: vertical group formations based on differentiations cut across the horizontal class lines based on property and prestige. The four most important vertical walls of separation are descent, religion, color, and length of settlement. They are so decisive in American life because the horizontal prestige system is powerless against them. One cannot, with money, buy another skin color or different forefathers. The constant operation of the ethnic walls of separation makes an absurdity of the idea of "the melting pot." Imponderable sentiments of superiority and inferiority come into play between the ethnic groups. Equality—and this may be instructive as regards human nature—has not led to fraternal unity, in which a man is distinguished only by his particular place, at a given time, in the general upward striving, but to a prestige system, in which the unveiled urge for distinction from one's fellows is the rule.

It is a discordant process. In the enjoyment of a high standard of living, America is becoming ever more egalitarian, but the reverse side of the same socio-historical process is that, as regards everything else, America is becoming proportionately more differentiated internally.

Americans are practically nomads in their vast country. They are, for the most part, lost in the huge economic organizations, which at the same time provide the security of a social framework. They stand apart from each other in the apparatus of production and distribution which, while it bene-ficently belches out goods, has also become mechanized and bureaucratized. Consequently, they try by means of status, real or artificial prestige, which they strive after by fair means or foul, to establish that sense of personal value without which a man cannot, it seems, or will not, lead a meaningful life, however blessed he may be with worldly goods. Under a mantle of egalitarianism, the indefatigable and inventive human spirit has created what is often a very subtle gradation of assertiveness, whereby men are led to say that they are not merely equal but equally different.

10.

A Reversed Theory of the Leisure Class

THE view most commonly expressed by American students of the problem of leisure is this: since the Fall of man, work has been the content of human existence, and civilizations and societies have been founded on the fact that man is at least a worker, if not a downright slave. Historically speaking, only small groups have been able to escape this fate and, by their privileged position in regard to leisure, have been identified as "upper classes." Now, however, a new era is opening. For the first time since the Fall, the alluring and disturbing possibility is looming that society as a whole, and not just the upper class, will become a "leisure class." As America moves toward a classless society, it becomes apparent that the most priceless privilege of former upper classes, the possession of a leisure exempt from all obligation to work, may pass to all the members of this highly industrialized society.

It is a prospect which fills some observers with the intoxicating feeling that America is on the way to bringing about culture in the Aristotelian sense of the wise use of leisure. Others are haunted by the gloomy picture of a nation intellectually and morally disintegrating from boredom and stupefied by commercialized entertainment. Few who have seriously concerned themselves with the problem of the future of work, play and leisure—and an increasing number of economists, union leaders, social scientists and philosophers of civilization are doing so—will dispute that in this field modern society will have to face a formidable challenge.

The dark shadow of collective boredom is already perceptible. The rise in productivity resulting from automation and the peaceful utilization of atomic energy has tremendously hastened the process of shortening the work week, a process which began with the industrial revolution. The five-day, forty-hour week is general throughout America, with its long two-day weekend. In February, 1962, the electricians' union in New York even managed to secure a contract providing for a twenty-five-hour week.

At the end of the nineteenth century, the work week was still seventy hours. In 1900, the sixty-hour week became general. In the nineteen thirties, Saturday afternoon became a half-day off. Now, the forty-hour week is the rule. But output, in terms of the individual worker, is 240 per cent higher today than it was when the seventy-hour week was in force. How fast this release from work will proceed depends on the speed at which industry is transformed by automation and atomic power. But the four-day week will not be long in coming, and the process of reduction of work hours will not stop there. Powerful social forces have begun to drive society in the direction of constantly increasing leisure time. The unions are demanding that the time saved through increased productivity should benefit the workers; behind this demand there is of course the fear of workers being dismissed. Their contention is that the big concerns should cut not personnel but work hours.

At the session of its executive council in Bal Harbor, Florida, in February, 1962, organized labor called for a flexible work week to combat the unemployment resulting from automation. Labor has become increasingly fearful that automation and "cybernation" will turn out to be a social Frankenstein. According to President Kennedy, the "major domestic challenge of the sixties" is "to maintain full employment at a time when automation is replacing men." Whatever the solution to this Midas gift of automation, most people will work less and less, at any rate among the masses.

The negative side of the reduction in working hours is the alienation of the worker from what remains of his work, not only in the automated plants but also, and to almost the same degree, in the labyrinthine industrial bureaucracies to which the majority of all professional workers are yoked. The "dignity of labor" has become largely fictional. A writer, Harvey Swados, who worked on the assembly line of an automobile plant in order to gather material, makes some very revealing comments on this point. It came as a shock to him, he writes, to discover that the only unifying force among all these men, so different in ethnic origin, educational level and personal ambition, was their hatred of their work. Leisure therefore appears to the sociologists as the counterbalance created by the production system itself; the very fact that in that system all jobs are stereotyped, except at the top, makes leisure possible.

The prospect of a future where millions will work scarcely more than an hour a day, this infinity of spare time in which the individual will be plunged, to use at his discretion, has a blasphemous ring; it is as though mankind were proposing by its own unaided powers to return to the Garden of Eden. In its crudeness, it illuminates a process which is already under way, the inversion of the social system, the re-evaluation of standards through the collectivizing of leisure.

In 1899 Thorstein Veblen published his famous *Theory of the Leisure Class,* so often reprinted and reinterpreted. It was the first attempt in America, in this society which theoretically, if not in practice, is so egalitarian, to establish a social classification, to discover a scale of social prestige, of "status." Veblen, a second-generation American of Norwegian descent, was frustrated in his university career. From personal experience he knew the pitiless distinctions existing in the American democracy. He placed the notion of leisure at the center of his investigation. This outsider, who could describe the upper class of his time with wit and sarcasm, and who was the first to reveal its "status" structure, evolved the sociological theory of leisure, from which expressions such as "conspicuous leisure," "leisure class," and "conspicuous consumption," have passed into common parlance. In a country without aristocratic tradition, the free disposal of one's time, and its disposal in a particular way, specifically by "conspicuous consumption" as a status symbol, became the badge of the new aristocracy. Veblen brought this value system into the open precisely by rejecting it.

Even if the social reality on which he built his heretical teaching has not so much disappeared as been overlaid by new groupings, it remains a fact that at one time, around the turn of the century, the ostentatious enjoyment of leisure was the specifically American badge of nobility. Only against this background can one really grasp the significance of a situation unprecedented in history, where the enjoyment of leisure will fall into the laps of the masses, whether they like it or not, as a consequence of technological progress.

The depth of the transformation, the strangeness of the ways of modern capitalism may be inferred from the change which has taken place in the position of leisure within the last fifty years. Nothing is more illuminating in this respect than to reread what Veblen wrote about the upper classes of his day. The reality from which he drew his theories was constituted by the newly founded millionaire dynasties, such as the Vanderbilts, Goulds, and Harrimans. Their style of living furnished him with the raw material for his view of the upper class.

Concealing his indignation, with difficulty, behind a professional sociological style, Veblen portrayed a class whose prestige lay in the display of ostentatious idleness. "Conspicuous abstention from labor becomes the conventional mark of superior pecuniary achievement." Such "conspicuous abstention from labor" expresses itself, in his very broad definition of lei-

sure, not only in upper class etiquette, in the observance of social rules regarding clothing, carriages, mansions, furniture,
hunting, sports and games, the possession of fashionable ani-
mals and race horses, art collections and books, but also in the
study of the classics and refined speech.

It is astonishing to observe these components of leisure reappearing, now, at the other end of the social scale. Veblen's
theory of the upper class as a leisure class is turned upside
down in this second part of the twentieth century in America.
The lower income groups now work less than the people in
positions of responsibility. Their leisure requirements are
already keeping the manufacturers of leisure products busier
than the requirements of the wealthy. As Russell Lynes has
put it, most Americans are now "part-time idle rich." The
"American way of life," in his view, consists precisely in the
counterbalancing of work and leisure for practically everyone.
Only one-third of the class which served Veblen as a model
still lives on unearned income. But even this third does not
indulge in "conspicuous consumption" as a status symbol—
unless the patronage of the great foundations can be considered a more refined version of the same thing.

What the new classless beneficiaries of leisure have yet to
learn from the former upper class is how to be carefree in the
enjoyment of their leisure. The American attitude to idleness
is considerably more complex than Veblen realized. He was
so busy ridiculing the rich, particularly their wives, that he
altogether overlooked the fact that their way of life meant
breaking with their Puritan heritage. For the leisure of the
very rich, at the turn of the century, was possible only because
of the tireless labor of the Puritan bourgeoisie which had
preceded it and still continued. American capitalism received
its strongest impetus from the work ethos of the Calvinistic
belief in predestination. Because, as Max Weber puts it,
"worldly professional work was used as the appropriate means
of shaking off the effects of religious anxiety," the possibility

of its contrary arose: first leisure for Veblen's upper class and now, still more paradoxically, leisure for all.

If the leisure of the millionaires between 1890 and 1930 was based on the work of the wealthy Puritan middle class, today the leisure of the lower and middle income groups is based on the work of the managerial class. Leisure has spread downward from the apex of the pyramid, and the intensity of work has risen upward; in this process the Puritan scale of values has been abandoned, or, at least, seems to have been abandoned.

The Puritan glorification of work, epitomized in Benjamin Franklin's *Advice to Young Tradesmen,* which was linked with a metaphysics of success, is no longer formative in personal philosophy, even in that of the young executive. Scientific investigations, as well as a series of novels about the world of business, have shown that hard work is no longer regarded as the content of life, success no longer as the principal aim. On the contrary, the reversal of values goes so far that the young executive feels a certain guilt when he violates the rules of the "well-rounded life"—the new ideal.

As William H. Whyte suggests in his *The Organization Man,* social ethics have taken the place of Protestant ethics. And according to social ethics, the goal of success is subordinated to the goal of being "well rounded." To desire success too intensely is regarded as antisocial. Whyte was able to gather so much material in suburbia about the reluctance to display success by material means that he used the Veblen phrase in reverse: "inconspicuous consumption." He notes that the young incumbents of managerial posts in the great firms avoid outdoing their neighbors in their personal spending, whether on cars, washing machines and other household appliances, on large houses, or on leisure products. Spending should not offend against the group spirit. According to European standards, however, such "inconspicuous consumption" can signify a high standard of living. But the important thing is that leisure and its use are not to arouse envy or demonstrate social superiority, but are integrated in a neighborly community life.

Would it not appear that the circumstances were most propitious for the emergence of an Aristotelian age of leisure for the masses? But why, then, have the psychiatrists less leisure in proportion as the rest of society has more? Can centuries of Puritanism be simply shaken off? Perhaps the truth is that Puritanism is trying to force its way in again through the back door. There is already a term for such veiled Puritanism —"fun morality"—meaning the strenuous pursuit of a good time. The idea is not only to have fun, in fact, by means of a preferably uninterrupted sequence of sports, games, films, theaters, picnics, and parties in one's free time and during vacations, but also to be always conscious of having fun, of having glorious fun. Fun as endeavor—that is the Puritan back door.

The ingenious David Riesman may have gone a little too far, in his *Individualism Reconsidered,* in comparing the modern suburban "explorers moving to the frontiers of consumption" with the old pioneers on the western frontier. The endeavor to find new forms of leisure in the suburban community will be and are less heroic. But his remark indicates that the process of adapting to new ways of life has its psychological price. Riesman describes the difficulties facing a wealthy suburbia which desires to practice the art of cultivated leisure. Parents are neurotic, children are unhappy, educationists and "mental hygienists," as they are called, have to be employed to look into the relationship between school and community. Music, riding, and dancing fill the free time of the children; the parents have enough time in the evening to talk with the schoolteachers about education, and also with their children, applying the advice received from the educationists, about the happenings of the day. In the family centered suburban society, which is regarded as the pattern for the future, the family is central in leisure too.

But why do the social "doctors" observe that the basic mood, especially among the women and children, is one of indeterminate fear? The answer again—as with eroticism—has some connection with the loss of spontaneity, with the tendency to rationalize the human, to make it too conscious. This self-consciousness is the foe of true leisure.

The learning of leisure is not made easier by the fact that the right people will not necessarily be the first to be in a position to cope with the bewildering gift of excess time. Not only do people work hardest at the managerial level, but the top executives and members of free professions bring home more inner tension than, for instance, the worker in a steel plant. Factory workers no longer come home physically exhausted, as in the past; on the contrary, even their unsatisfactory work day—unsatisfactory from the point of view of ethical content—has its built-in leisure in the form of rest periods, coffee breaks and lunch breaks. While the industrial worker's formerly murderous pace of work has slowed down and energies are therefore conserved for the increasing leisure time, there is an increasing frequency of deaths from heart condition among members of the free professions, particularly doctors and lawyers. The young executives are subjected to the kind of strains which have always been present in great administrations, which is what business organizations have become. Thus, the groups which should best be able to make creative use of free time are precisely those which have been least blessed with it.

The reversal of the leisure pyramid is tangibly expressed in the scale of spending on leisure products. More than half the outboard motors which have become so popular are bought by skilled workers, craftsmen, medium-salaried employees. Golf equipment is increasingly purchased at all levels, for even if the golf clubs are the walled citadels of social snobbery, anyone can play gratis on public golf courses. The sale of fishing tackle has doubled in the last ten-odd years because of the demand for the less expensive products. All this shows where the increase of leisure will lead. More and more people go in for golf, fishing, skiing, motorboating, and deep-sea diving (there are hundreds of deep-sea diving clubs). Some eighty million American tourists travel about their continent each year and spend more in the process, so it has been estimated, than the entire amount of the French national budget. Upper-class pursuits seep downward. Is there also a contrary movement? Edward Dutton, for instance, writes, in *Recreation,* that unskilled workers could emulate the English upper class of former times by concerning themselves with politics. Such an infusion of fresh blood from the factory would, he feels, further the democratic process. Sociologists, concerned with the advance of culture, are less sanguine.

Although there is now a great deal more active participation in sport instead of merely passive spectator participation at crowded sports centers, it has been established that up to eighty per cent of leisure time is spent before the television screen at home. Here, television reigns unchallenged (an inactive form of contemplation which Aristotle can hardly have had in mind when he recommended it as the content of wise leisure), interrupted, perhaps, by lawn mowing, car washing, amateur carpentry, or amateur painting of every conceivable object with foolproof paints. Here social problems begin to interlock. Without a constructive organization of leisure, there can be no counterbalancing of the loss of purpose provided by work; without a recasting of television, which threatens to become the dubious expression of a commercial society, leisure will be the captive of mere time-killing.

A solution to this problem is contained in a paper of the National Education Society on automation and education presented in 1962: "Our proposal calls for a redefinition of the work week. Given the historical trend toward a shorter week, we suggest that the present forty hours be maintained, but that only thirty-six hours be devoted to productive labor, with the remaining four hours given to education. The essential point is that the gain in productivity be recaptured for the personal growth of the individual . . ." Such ideas show that machines raise productivity so fast that millions of workers are in danger of being left behind without any meaningful existence—a situation particularly dangerous for the young, the drop-outs from high school (some one million annually), who are unschooled, unskilled and, thanks to automation, unemployed.

The dawning age of excess time can take unaccountable forms. Traditional concepts of time, that stuff of human existence, will perhaps have to be abandoned. One notion that will probably be given up, according to certain theorists, is that all men should work and rest at the same times. The automated factory will probably produce best if it is in operation around the clock. Workers will therefore have their "weekends" at quite different times on different days.

What will a "cybernated society" be like? Experts predict that what will be needed are trouble-crews to repair break-downs and highly sophisticated top management which is likely to be overworked. "The rest of us will be out of work or underworked."

The sophistication of taste, of living requirements, or habits, this very evident feature of American life in the last few years, is essentially a consequence of increasing leisure. In a society which so constantly and so deliberately observes itself, like a sick man his body, leisure develops its own type of dynamism. Commercial interests, as well as intellectual forces, stream into the vacuum. We shall see which is the stronger. The intellectuals themselves, when they deal with the prospects of the age of leisure, conclude for the most part on an optimistic note. Thus Clifton Fadiman, for instance, recalling that, in ancient Greece, leisure societies founded on slavery discovered a joyous, spontaneous, but conscious intellectualism, on the basis of which they created a unique civilization, suggests that the American society, which will be a leisure society founded on the machine, could create something similar if it so wished. Robert Bendiner, writing in the *Reporter,* is more cautious: "Much evidence might be cited to show that the nation is at least carrying on a flirtation with the Muses which can reasonably be expected to deepen with time and experience." He headed his article: "Could you stand the four-day week?" How much unencumbered time can a whole society stand? Can it, without injury to itself, forego, on an as-yet-unimaginable scale, the "privilege" of earning its bread by the sweat of its brow? This is a new problem in human history.

Index

Index prepared by Marion H. Downey

The Author and His Book

HERBERT VON BORCH *was born in Swatow, China, in 1909, where his father was then serving as a German diplomat to China. He studied at the Universities of Berlin and Frankfurt and in 1933 he received his Doctor of Philosophy from the University of Heidelberg, graduating summa cum laude. Presently the author lives in Washington and is the American correspondent for the German paper* Die Welt. *He is a member of The National Press Club, Washington, D.C. In 1959, he was awarded the* Joseph Drexel Preis, *a German equivalent of the Pulitzer Prize, for his reporting from Washington. Founder of the German foreign affairs magazine* Aussenpolitik, *he has also been an editorial writer for the* Frankfurter Allgemeine Zeitung, *and the contributor of several radio lectures about life and politics in the United States. He has been a writer for such American magazines as* The New Republic *and* Confluence, *a Harvard magazine. Mr. von Borch has traveled all over the world and speaks German, English and Italian, with a reading knowledge of French and Spanish. His books include*

The Divine Right of Kings *(Junker and Duennhaupt, 1934)*, Authority and Resistance *(J. C. B. Mohr, 1954), and* Kennedy, the New Style and World Politics *(R. Piper and Co., 1961)*, *all published in Germany.*

THE UNFINISHED SOCIETY *(Hawthorn Books, 1962) was set in type by Harry Sweetman Typesetting Corp., New York City. Presswork and binding were done by Montauk Book Manufacturing Co., Inc. The body type is Granjon, designed for linotype under the supervision of George W. Jones and named after the French type designer, Robert Granjon.*

A HAWTHORN BOOK

DATE DUE

MAY 17 '63			
MAY 22 '64			
GAYLORD			PRINTED IN U.S.A.